STRONG ENOUGH

COMPILED BY **Jane Rowan**

First published in 2026 by Eating Disorders Families Australia (EDFA)

Produced by OSTRICH180

© 2026 Eating Disorders Families Australia

www.edfa.org.au

Cover design by Catucci Design
Internal design by Independent Ink
Typeset in Montserrat by Post Pre-press Group, Brisbane

A catalogue record for this book is available from the National Library of Australia

ISBN 978-1-7645677-0-1 (paperback)
ISBN 978-1-7645677-1-8 (epub)
ISBN 978-1-7645677-2-5 (kindle)

We acknowledge the sponsors for this project.
Helen and David Hains Foundation.

Contents

Disclaimer

This book contains personal stories and reflections shared by individual carers who have supported a loved one experiencing an eating disorder. Each contributor speaks solely from their own experience. The insights, opinions, treatment descriptions, and recovery pathways presented in these chapters are personal to the authors and may not reflect the views of the editors, publishers, or Eating Disorders Families Australia (EDFA).

The information provided is for general understanding, encouragement, and education only. It is **not** intended replace medical, psychological, nutritional, or therapeutic advice. Eating disorders are complex medical and mental health conditions, and each individual's needs are unique. Readers should always seek guidance from qualified healthcare professionals for diagnosis, treatment decisions, and crisis support.

While every effort has been made to ensure accuracy at the time of publication, medical knowledge and best practice evolve, and approaches may vary across clinicians, services, and countries. Neither the authors, EDFA, nor the publisher accepts responsibility for any loss, harm, or adverse outcomes arising from the use or interpretation of information contained in this book.

Some chapters contain descriptions of distressing experiences including references to suicide. Reader discretion is advised.

If you or someone you care for is in immediate danger or experiencing a medical or mental health crisis, please call 000 or contact Lifeline on 13 11 14.

Foreword

Jane Rowan, Executive Director,
Eating Disorders Families Australia

When my daughter, Charley, became unwell with anorexia, our world quietly fell apart. Food – once a symbol of family and connection – became a battleground. Every meal, every morsel, carried the weight of fear, love, and desperate hope. Nothing could have prepared us for this invisible enemy, or for the helplessness of watching my child fight an illness that so few truly understand.

Our story, like those of so many families and carers, is one of persistence, advocacy, and love that refuses to give up. There were moments when I questioned whether we would ever find our way back to peace – yet somehow, through determination, time, and relentless hope, we did. That journey forever changed the way I see the power of carers.

When I became Executive Director of Eating Disorders Families Australia (EDFA), I carried those lessons with me. I knew the quiet, unseen story of carers – parents, partners, siblings, friends – was something the world needed to hear. *Strong Enough* was born from that conviction. It is a book for every carer who has stood at the edge of despair and chosen, again and again, to keep believing in recovery.

These pages hold stories of heartbreak and healing, of ordinary people who found extraordinary courage. What makes them truly remarkable is not just the honesty with which they are told, but the generosity behind them – carers sharing their most private pain, with the blessing of their loved ones, in the hope their stories might light the way for someone else. At a time when eating disorders are still surrounded by misunderstanding and stigma, this act of openness is both courageous and transformative.

They remind us that carers are not merely bystanders – they are lifelines. They are, indeed, the frontline of recovery. Their love, though often unacknowledged, is a powerful force for survival and, ultimately, healing.

It has been my dream since joining EDFA to create something that captures the reality of caring – not only the heartbreak and exhaustion, but also the fierce, enduring love that carries us through. Its creation has only been possible through the extraordinary generosity of the Helen and David Hains Foundation, whose belief in the power of storytelling turned that dream into reality. Their support has allowed these voices – honest, raw, and profoundly moving – to reach the world.

My gratitude also goes to Charli Fels, who through her own, different caring journey, brought immense empathy, wisdom, and artistry to this project. Her compassionate guidance helped our authors shape their stories with truth and tenderness.

To every carer who shared their story: thank you for your courage, your vulnerability, and your trust. And to every reader who recognises a piece of themselves within these pages: please know that you are not alone. You are seen. You are valued.

You are – and always have been – strong enough.

CHAPTER 1

Strong Enough

By Andrea and Bryce Wilson

Opening

This is our family's journey as we fell into the dark abyss of fear and anxiety that is depression and anorexia. We wrote this story together during the fight to save our child as she battled a serious and deadly disease that inflicts damage every day. To any parent, carer, clinician, or friend, we hope you find this chapter informative, but in the end, we share this deeply personal journey as an insight, maybe as a support to find a way out of the darkness, but most importantly as a message of strength and hope.

In the words of our daughter, Kennedy, "Please take this from a person who knows what it is like. Know you can't just snap out of it, know that sometimes you need to seek further help, but most importantly know that you can break the cycle."

The Darkest Night

31 January 2024. It's late. We've been waiting at the hospital for hours, first in the emergency department and now in the paediatric ward. The heart monitor is screeching again. Her heart rate is too low, and we've been moved from the paediatric general ward into high care. Bradycardia (slow heart rate) is dangerous and silent. We didn't know our child was at risk until she was admitted, and it's clear now that her heart has been struggling for a while.

There seems to be more and more people in the room as the minutes tick by. Why is she so cold? The room temperature is ramped up, more heated blankets applied, now an inflatable hot air cover is hooked up. The nasogastric tube that was force-feeding vital nutrients directly into her stomach must be switched off due to her vulnerable condition. She needs more fluids. Each attempt to insert another cannula into her dehydrated veins seems to fail. The IV machine can't deliver fluids fast enough. Eventually, a nurse unhooks the machine, grabs a massive syringe, and starts manually pushing fluids in. More medical staff are filing in.

The heart monitor alarm goes off again.

There is a conversation going on in the corridor. The young doctors are discussing whether to contact the on-call supervisor for advice on what to do next. The intensive care staff will need to be informed if a transfer is coming. Do they have a bed?

It's after 2 a.m. The supervisor's response comes back – wait another 20 minutes before transferring to ICU …

And finally, her blood pressure improves,
her heart rate is stabilising.
The IV infusion pump is dripping calmly again.
The NG feeding tube is switched back on.
We survive another day.

Just focusing on surviving the next 24 hours – that is the way it had been for months, and that was the way it would be for many more months to come.

The Slide into Teenage Depression and Disordered Eating

How did we get here? Reflecting back on daycare, kindergarten, and primary school, they were not easy. Every year of care and schooling had its challenges. Whether it was a school excursion, a sleepover, or a substitute teacher, there were often tears, upset, or just not being able to get there. Our daughter excelled academically, but like her mother (and grandparents), she has always been anxious and struggled in social situations. The first year of high school brought some challenges, but we thought that some additional support to work on social skills would be enough to navigate the changing dynamics of high school.

We were wrong. As parents with limited understanding of children's mental health issues, we did not fully comprehend her level of anxiety and, later, depression. Our kind, compliant daughter was trying to let us know that she was not doing well, and we tentatively explored some generic counselling. But little did we know, we were in another league.

Our daughter was withdrawing further and further; she was regularly sliding into dark episodes of hopelessness. In hindsight, we understand that this was clinical depression, and our hearts ache to recall the loneliness and self-harm that followed.

We hoped things would improve following an autism diagnosis and changing to a new school. We were wrong again, but we kept trying. Not long after she had turned 14, we began to notice that she wasn't eating her lunch at school, she would go without breakfast sometimes, she stopped having milk in coffee, she ate pizza with a knife and fork, broke up bread into small pieces, ordered fries and only ate a few. At the same time, baking became an obsession. The kitchen was heaving with spectacular, multi-layered, elaborate cakes. Sadly, most went uneaten.

We were not fully aware of the significance of all these signs, but perhaps we should have seen that what was in front of us was definitely a disordered eating situation. With so much food noise, relentlessly everywhere, it can be overwhelming. Online, at school, at home – the constant pressure to look, eat, and exercise a certain way. We talked too much about calories and weight, and we carelessly threw around comments about physical appearance. What we know now is that there are no "bad" calories when you are trying to keep a child alive.

In Kennedy's words, "Many people have gone through a period of disordered eating, but the depth of an eating disorder is different. Every person has a different experience, but the best way to understand an eating disorder is that it is an addiction. Most people understand the high of not having that extra biscuit, doing some additional exercise, or choosing the healthier option. It is a pleasant feeling, and when you have nothing else to feel, or your life is chaotic or stressful, it becomes an addictive sense of control. So, you do it again: you skip breakfast, go further into the day without eating, and don't have the extra slice of bread. You do it again and again. And suddenly, like a drug, it's not the high your body and mind chase; it's just the action, and you can't fathom going without your drug. No matter how much someone says to 'just eat' or asks, 'why would you do that?', it doesn't change anything. You obsess – all you can think about is when you can next restrict or when you let yourself slip and eat."

Diagnosis and Desperation

December 2023. We planned a family holiday, hoping that a change of scene, new experiences, and a visit with friends could turn things around. We knew our daughter was underweight and anxious, but she was excited about something for the first time in a long time. So, we flew off – full of misplaced optimism.

Unfortunately, the distress of eating didn't disappear, and the self-loathing post-eating only increased. Her eating disorder had a stranglehold. Her undernourished brain was mistakenly giving her positive feedback for restricting; she was becoming paranoid about hidden calories, angry with our insistence on nourishment, and aggressively obstructive to our attempts to seek help. In her starved mind, every morsel was a gross overindulgence and had to be punished. All attempts at logical persuasion or parental instruction were futile.

It was clear that our daughter was sick, but we didn't yet know just how sick. Being such a long way from home meant it wasn't easy to get help. Sincere thanks go to our dear friends stationed at the embassy, to the Butterfly Helpline, and to our staunch, dependable Aussie GP who calmly guided us through those distraught phone calls at all hours.

We were able to secure a telehealth appointment with a specialist and, with great trepidation, recounted all that had transpired. It was 3 a.m., a session with just Mum and Dad, packed into a small hotel bathroom so we didn't wake her. The specialist was in no doubt; the pattern was clear – "Your child has anorexia nervosa." A moment no parent ever forgets.

We began frantically scouring every information source in an attempt to understand this unfathomable disease. As scientists, we turned to the peer-reviewed literature, and what a stark picture it painted. Anorexia nervosa has the highest mortality rate of all mental illnesses. Treatment pathways varied, and success was mixed. FBT (family-based treatment) appeared to be the recommended best practice. We began reading accounts from those with lived experience. We searched frantically for

organisations that could help, clinicians, treatment programs –
the desperation set in.

We felt like we were in free fall and knew we did not have
long before our daughter would be too unwell to travel. We
feared being stuck overseas and knew that we needed to
connect with the Australian health system as soon as possible.
Again, thanks go to family and friends who supported us as we
made the dash to get our girl safely back home.

In Kennedy's words, "Understanding what it is like to be in
the mind of a person with an eating disorder is almost impossible. When you are deep in the disease, you don't want to talk
about it, and even after, it is hard to describe."

Back Home, Things Go From Bad to Worse

Apart from the deep sadness of what was happening to our
daughter, now it was even clearer that every day mattered, every
calorie mattered, and every meal mattered. Once we got back
home, we began a gruelling daily routine of struggling to get
something eaten. Starting with tiny portions of breakfast, a piece
of bread for lunch, and maybe getting in a fraction of dinner.

We kept up with the telehealth appointments and FBT
sessions, followed by tears, anger, and hopelessness. We followed
the instructions and fought the battle. But to no avail – the
pattern of restricting continued. Eating was being dictated by
the despotic, unattainable rules of the eating disorder. Every
day, we were slipping further behind. Not sure we have ever
cried as hard or been more frightened of failing. But we were
determined to keep going because there was no other option.

Fortunately, we had the support of a compassionate
and knowledgeable GP with previous experience of eating

disorders. Dr W was no-nonsense and had cared for our family for many years. We all trusted her. She kept a close eye on our daughter's medical stability and gave us every chance to turn things around at home. But it was clear that our child was becoming weaker with each day. Every weigh-in showed more and more losses. Although we knew it was coming, we still felt the shock when our GP told us that we needed to get our daughter to hospital. Her life was at risk. Hospital admission is frightening, but we understand now that it can be what's required to halt the decline.

In Kennedy's words, "The disease feeds off everything you do; the more starved you are, the less logical you think. You are locked in the eating disorder. It can be hard to understand, and you can't help if you don't understand."

47 Days

We feared hospital and so were doing everything to avoid that path. But as it turned out, hospital was actually where we needed to be to start refeeding. Despite the trauma of that first, darkest night, there was some respite in being enveloped by the hospital system. We succumbed to the regimented routine of scheduled meals, nasogastric tubing, hourly observations, regular blood tests, and multi-disciplinary team (MDT) meetings twice a week.

We passed the time with chess, reading, streaming, baking videos, board games, and even daggy free-to-air TV. It was a grinding parental routine, day after day after day. Snatching snippets of sleep on the scratchy hospital room lounges, driving back and forth to the hospital multiple times a day. We put together a soundtrack to keep us going, achingly sad but somehow galvanising. Thanks to Dido ("White Flag") and Ian Hickie (*The Devil You Knew*) for getting us through those lonely, late-night drives.

But what we were going through was nothing compared to the nightmare that our daughter endured throughout this time. Her tiny, defeated frame perched in the sterile hospital bed still haunts us. Pale, still, dark rings of exhaustion under her eyes. Connected to whirring and beeping machines, tubes running into her nose, her arms.

Then the wheelchair would arrive to collect her for the next ordeal. Time to enter the torturous "white room" for another mealtime, to battle the demons again. Her quiet courage, her stoic determination, steels us for another day.

Treating the Whole Person

FBT is a tried and tested method to treat eating disorders in Australia and overseas. We understand that practitioners have refined this program to be best practice. It was our strategy to listen carefully to the clinicians treating our daughter and to focus on evidence-based approaches.

But we also remembered the lived experience and advice from our support network ("focus on mental health as well as physical health"). So right from the start, we pushed for psychiatric support. The standard response is medical stability first. We accepted this and were guided by the experienced practitioners. But we kept coming back to mental health, kept asking for consultations with the psychiatric team, who happened to be just next door.

When the time came to start the healing process for our daughter's renourished brain, it was a relief to find a competent and proactive mental health team ready to engage. The importance of connecting with the right clinician at the right time can't be overstated. After so many failed attempts at mental health treatment, considering so many painful disappointments, it took an enormous amount of courage for our daughter to give this one more try. Thanks to Bridgette for being that special person who made the difference, who was able to nurture our damaged and traumatised child, to build a fragile trust, just enough to make one more attempt.

Hospital routines and rules do not easily accommodate the needs of autistic patients. Constant advocacy was necessary to ensure bespoke care was available. But we thank the MDT crew, including the hospital staff who provided remote consultation, for listening to our concerns and being willing to adjust. For example, some neurodivergent patients will never be able to tolerate certain flavours and textures. It can be difficult for clinicians to accept that it is not the eating disorder speaking and that flexibility is required to tailor recovery for specific patient needs. In our case, the MDT allowed us to bring in food from home to overcome the limitations of hospital cuisine. This willingness to listen and try different approaches allowed us to shorten the length of admission time.

These tentative steps forward did not come without conflicts, setbacks, and mistakes. The decision to administer antidepressant drugs to our child was an extremely difficult one. We carefully considered the scientific literature, consulted with medical experts, psychologists, and psychiatrists, discussed it with those who have lived experience, and listened to our child. Medication may not be the right pathway for everyone, but in our case, the advice of clinicians to prescribe SSRIs was lifesaving.

The Hard Work Has to Keep Going

When we got home from hospital, the hard work continued. Week after week, then fortnight after fortnight for 18 months, we would grind through the challenging outpatient appointments and home-based tasks. And we were all so very tired, worn out. Through this journey, it is understandable to feel overwhelming fear that you may lose your child. To feel anxiety that, despite your best efforts, you may not prevail. But onwards and upwards.

With our psychologist's help, we doggedly ploughed on with regular FBT sessions – confronting fear foods, enduring weigh-ins, tolerating exposure to anxiety-provoking situations, and tackling the difficult parts of mental health conversations. We sincerely thank the dedicated staff at the community mental health service for your steadfast care and support, pushing us to do the hard work and being there, in the public system, to take on a young person with an eating disorder.

Inherent in the FBT treatment approach is a questioning of parenting styles and unpacking of risk factors. This feels like judgement; it is reasonable to be defensive. We sometimes wondered what we could have done differently. At times, it's hard to believe that you are in this tunnel, panicking as you free fall, grasping to come to grips with the trauma as you watch your child every day, losing weight, losing condition, sliding further.

This is when the support system is critical. It's sometimes hard to ask for help, but in this hellhole, every resource at your disposal must be mobilised to save your child – networks, friends, colleagues, clinicians, EDFA, the Butterfly Foundation, GPs, psychiatrists, psychologists, dieticians, local MPs, other parents, charities, whatever it takes.

We are forever grateful to the caring friends who quietly and generously wrapped around us to provide words of support, who regularly checked in, dropped home-cooked meals on our doorstep, shared books to help pass the hours in hospital, stood back when we needed them to and leaned in when we asked. Particularly to those who shared their lived experience as carers, whose empathetic, loving, and non-judgemental listening was so important for us to feel that we were not a bad family, not bad parents, and who gave us reassurance that, with support, we would get through.

Stigma, Silence, and Shame

The number of people who die each year due to eating disorders is higher than the annual national road toll. Yet, there continues to be ignorance and misunderstanding of eating disorders and mental health more broadly. Being ill with an eating disorder is not like a broken arm, where people come and sign your cast; the anguish of mental health is almost always hidden, and it is not something we easily share.

As parents and carers, we need to show strength and compassion, let our young people know that we have their backs, no matter what. That is why we are working with EDFA to contribute to this book. We want to raise awareness about how this cruel disease impacts ordinary families every day. And we want to talk about hope, to show that it is possible to emerge from this hellish place.

Closing

Unfortunately, there is no clear step-by-step guide to recovery; there is no "mission accomplished" moment as you battle out of anorexia. But there are important victories along the way. We have made it into remission. Climbing out of that dark place wasn't a solo journey; we built a team. We were "all in". We listened to other carers, were evidence-based, leaned on every relationship, and insisted on treatment of the whole person.

All of the above is not to say that every journey ends with remission, and to those parents who are still battling – we see you, we know you are giving your all, that you are in that hell, and we are here collectively for you. Know that you are strong enough.

CHAPTER 2

The Life Plan – Taking Control, Not Being Controlled

By Kristine Rawlinson, with permission of and final word by Sam Furze

The Comfort of a Plan

From the time we are children, most of us are taught that having a plan is the mark of responsibility. Plans are meant to give direction, structure, and comfort. They keep chaos at bay. For me, my life plan was clear from an early age.

I would excel at school. I would graduate from university and find a stable, respected profession. I would meet a wonderful husband, build a beautiful home, and raise at least two high-achieving children who reflected our shared ambition and talent.

It wasn't just a vague dream; I had it mapped out step by step, like a recipe for success.

And, for a while, life seemed to reward my careful planning. I finished high school as dux and valedictorian. By the age of 26, I was already managing a statewide team of therapists as a speech pathologist. By my early 30s, I was designing models of care, leading policy reforms, and managing partnerships in the state government disability services sector, and had three university qualifications to my name. Each milestone ticked another box on the plan.

When I met Neal, he didn't fit the profile of the husband I had imagined. He was 13 years older, a confirmed bachelor at 46, and far from the polished picture of the partner I had "planned". But he was kind, surprising, and willing to embrace my plan to start a family quickly. That seemed like enough, and I was happy.

Within a year, we had moved to the country to start our idyllic new life on 20 acres. When I found out I was pregnant soon after, it felt as though the universe was conspiring to deliver on the life I had so carefully charted. Everything was falling neatly into place, and I was pretty damn smug about it.

When Reality Doesn't Match the Plan

The pregnancy that was meant to be glowing and Instagram-worthy (what did we do in those days, pre-Insta? It's hard to imagine!). I envisioned photo shoots in fields of sunflowers, featuring me and my baby bump in a tight black dress. Instead, my pregnancy became a medical ordeal. I was on crutches, sometimes in a wheelchair, dealing with pelvic instability and gestational diabetes so severe that acupuncture and insulin became part of my routine care.

By the time baby Sam arrived, I was exhausted and relieved. The struggles of pregnancy faded and became a distant memory as I basked in the joy of holding my tiny son. Yet even before I left the hospital, panic crept in. I remember lying awake the night before discharge, overwhelmed by the thought: "How am I supposed to keep this tiny human alive, let alone help him thrive?"

That moment marked the first crack in the illusion that my plan could protect me from fear or uncertainty.

Still, as Sam grew, I returned to my plan. I poured myself into parenthood with the same determination I had poured into my career. With my background in speech pathology and special education, I immersed him in language from day one. I used sign language. I read to him. I surrounded him with words and ideas. And it seemed to work. By an early age, Sam was identified as gifted. He was quirky, imaginative, and endlessly curious. This kid impressed everyone with his capacity to use his language and charm to convince people to do just about anything he wanted.

It wasn't unusual for him to strike up conversations with staff at shops in our small local community, completely charming them with his capacity to converse like an adult, despite being a toddler.

At the time, I mistook quirkiness for brilliance. His creative use of language, his colour-coded bath toys, his obsession with rules and routines. I celebrated all of it as proof of his uniqueness and intellect. In my mind, he was on track to fulfil the "mini-plan" I had for him: academic success, university, and a future of achievement.

But life has a way of testing the rigidity of plans.

Parenthood and the "Perfect Child" Plan

When Sam was four, his kinder teacher suggested he repeat a year. Her reasoning was gentle but clear. Although he was constantly playing, he rarely played with other children. Instead, he preferred to direct them into elaborate games governed by his own complicated rules. She even gave me a book called *Tricky Kids* and marked the chapter she thought fit Sam best: "The CEO".

I was offended at first. How dare she imply my brilliant child was difficult? But beneath my defensiveness was fear. I had the creeping sense that my carefully constructed plan might not fit the reality of who my child was.

This was the first of many reminders that when we try to impose our plan onto someone else's life, especially our children's, we risk missing who they truly are.

As Sam grew older, these cracks widened. He won academic awards but also endured bullying. He made friends but often came home in tears. I would open his lunchbox to find it was mostly untouched, and put it down to him not wanting to miss out on playing with others. There were mega meltdowns. Neal and I disagreed on how to deal with Sam's outbursts. I was a therapist, trained to see challenging behaviour as a form of communication – it was our challenge to work out what it was that he was trying to communicate. Neal was raised as one of five boys in the 1960s, where the approach to discipline could not have been more different.

I sensed something wasn't right and sought medical opinions, but doctors dismissed my concerns. To them, he was bright, charming, and articulate. To me, Sam was struggling in ways I couldn't quite name.

Still, I clung to the plan. If he could just keep achieving, if I could just keep scaffolding him, everything would work out. That's the lie we tell ourselves when we confuse control with care.

Crisis: The Shattering of the Plan

The real breaking point didn't come from Sam but from Neal. When Sam was eleven, Neal contracted meningococcal disease. Within weeks, our lives were turned upside down. We were told that Neal was either going to die or end up with a severe and complex disability.

Neal spent a month in a coma. His legs, fingers, and thumbs were amputated. Six strokes left him with a significant brain injury.

In the hallway of the ICU, a well-meaning relative told Sam,

"You're the man of the house now. You need to look after your family."

Those words lodged like a stone in his chest. For the next two years, Sam slept with a cricket bat beside his bed, ready to protect us. He lost weight, developed dark circles under his eyes, and began skipping classes to spend time with the school counsellor. Childhood was stripped away and replaced with fear and responsibility.

There were, however, moments of joy. Sam played the role of the Artful Dodger in *Oliver!* He performed at a community theatre production and then took on lead roles in other shows, wowing audiences. He had a close group of friends that were, and still remain, a source of support to him and, ultimately, our family.

But he carried a silent burden that no child should.

When Neal eventually returned home, Sam summed up the heartbreaking truth: "My dad died. That man there is not him." The father-son relationship was broken in ways that could not be repaired.

By the time Sam was 16, the cracks turned into a cliff edge. One night at 4 a.m., he came into my bedroom, crying. "Mum, I have to tell you something. I just tried to kill myself, and I couldn't even get that right. I hate my life, and I need help."

In that moment, the life plan I had clung to crumbled entirely.

Letting Go of the Old Plan

I rushed Sam into the mental health system, where we discovered what professionals had missed for years: he was autistic, and he had an eating disorder, avoidant/restrictive food intake disorder (ARFID). I will never forget the specialist saying to me, "How could you, as a speechie, not know your own son was autistic?" The grief and guilt that I already felt at this stage grew exponentially and then hit a crescendo that became anger – but not until later. We had more immediate concerns. Sam was in "brain starvation", and his heart was under a dangerous strain. We were sent to the hospital immediately to see a paediatrician for admission.

This was during the height of COVID, when hospitals were stretched to breaking point. It was like a scene from *M*A*S*H*, and Sam was completely freaked out by all the people and the hospital noises (of course, remember our family has a complex history with hospitals).

We were sent home (without ever seeing the paediatrician, who was too busy) and placed under the supervision of a refeeding program and family-based therapy (FBT). The weight of responsibility fell on me. I became both mother and nurse, ally and adversary, as I pushed him to eat foods that terrified him.

It was exhausting and heartbreaking. I blamed myself for not seeing the signs earlier, for being distracted by Neal's illness, for failing to live up to the impossible standard of the perfect mother.

But amid the chaos, there was a turning point. I honestly can't remember whether it was a health professional or someone from Sam's school who asked us both what we wanted Sam to achieve by the end of the year. Sam answered first: "Mum will want me to finish high school with top marks." I followed with: "I just want Sam to live."

We looked at each other in shock. In that moment, the truth was exposed. My old plan had been about achievement. His assumption was that I still valued grades above all else. But what I wanted, what I needed, was for him to be alive, to reclaim joy, to simply be.

That moment gave both of us permission to drop the crushing expectations.

Building a New Kind of Plan – Agency and Choice

The paradox was clear: freedom came when we let go of rigid planning. Instead of being controlled by a script, we could co-create a new path, one built around Sam's needs, strengths, and choices.

We found a new GP, Trisha, who became our anchor. She saw Sam weekly, providing us with steady support, especially through times when we felt like the rug was pulled out from under us (e.g. when Sam had to be hospitalised under the direction of his psychiatrist). We built a team of neuro-affirming professionals who listened to us, rather than dictating and judging. We drew on NDIS funding and private health insurance to fill the gaps left by an overstretched public system.

Meals remained a battlefield, but we stopped fighting for variety and instead focused on consistency. His "safe foods" list, which will come as no surprise to those of you in the same boat, includes chicken nuggets, chips, pasta, brownies, garlic bread, chocolate, and soft drinks. While this might horrify dieticians, his blood tests showed no deficiencies. Progress didn't look like kale salads and green smoothies. It looked like survival, stability, and slow weight gain.

He eats at his computer desk. We don't eat around a dinner table as a family. That was heavily judged by lots of "experts". Ours is not a "typical" family. That scenario does not suit us. We pick our battles.

School changed, too. Traditional structures were too rigid, so Sam shifted to a neuro-affirming education provider, completing his high school requirements through passion projects such as analysing the historical accuracy of video games. His overall score wasn't the dux-level result my old plan demanded, but it was enough. And more importantly, it was his.

Gradually, agency shifted into his hands. He negotiated with his GP about appointment frequency. He found a psychiatrist he liked, and they decided to trial medication that supported both appetite and mental health. He learned to manage his energy, even if that sometimes meant staying up gaming until 4 a.m.

It wasn't perfect, but it was ours.

Lessons for Anyone with a Life Plan

Looking back, I see the danger of rigid planning. Plans promise safety but can become prisons. They can blind us to reality, shame us into silence, and trap us in the expectations of others.

The greatest lesson I've learned is that true planning is about agency. It's important to have a plan, but who's in control, what is the purpose of that control, and when do we need to let go of that control?

For parents, it means recognising when we are writing our children's story instead of helping them write their own. For professionals, it means supporting families without imposing one-size-fits-all models. For individuals, it means asking: "Whose plan am I living?"

It's not that planning is bad. It's that plans must be flexible, adaptable, and human. They should bend under pressure, not shatter lives when reality shifts.

The Gift of an Unfinished Plan

The night Sam came to me in despair was the worst night of my life. But it was also the beginning of a new way of living. A way where survival mattered more than grades, where joy mattered more than appearances, and where agency mattered more than adherence to anyone else's expectations.

Today, Sam is at university, studying one subject at a time, slowly building a life on his terms. He is eating more, living more, laughing more. And I am no longer trying to control the plan. I am walking alongside him as he creates his own.

The life plan changes. Sometimes it collapses. Sometimes it becomes unrecognisable. But the true measure of a good life isn't how closely we stick to the plan. It's whether we get to choose, to adapt, and to live with freedom and agency.

For me, for Sam, and for anyone wrestling with the tension between control and surrender, the invitation is simple:

Make a plan if you like. But make sure it is your plan. And when life demands a change, don't cling to the script. Pick up the pen, take control, and write the next chapter yourself.

Kristine's Top 5 Tips

1. **Get chickens** – they will eat all the uneaten food and reward you with eggs!

2. **Boundaries** – family and friends will have advice, opinions, etc. You may need to place some boundaries on relationships for a while so you can focus on supporting your young person.

3. **Be the cheerleader, not the captain** – remind yourself that you are doing this because you are your young person's biggest fan and you want them to be well, not because they are the problem. Sometimes, some treatment approaches can put you in these adversarial roles. That's no good for either of you.

4. **Forget what other people think** – no one knows and will fully appreciate the heartbreak, the exhaustion, the guilt, the grief, the worry, the desperation, the anger, and the fear that you are carrying. Focus on looking after your young person and yourself, and don't ever blame yourself for your child's eating disorder.

5. **Connect with others** – this might be with others who have kids with eating disorders. This might be with others who are in your local book club. This might be with others who like yoga or pole dancing, or darts. Just stay connected so you don't forget who you are. It's too easy to throw everything into "fighting the eating disorder". It's a David and Goliath battle, which usually goes on for years, so you need stamina and support. Making your whole life about fighting the eating disorder is not sustainable. Find a way to build the fight into your life, but still have a life.

Sam – The Final Word

Plans are hard, just a plain, simple fact.

No matter how hard you try, no matter what you think you've prepared for, there will always be something in life that you just never planned for.

Sometimes there's a loud crash that can shake everything up instantly, but sometimes there's a slow-burning crack in the hourglass of life, causing pressure to build, and more and more cracks to appear over time, until finally, it breaks.

Plans will break, bend, and are never 100% reliable. But there is at least one constant that I've found. The greatest thing you can have in these times is someone who cares about you. Not a doctor who tells you it'll get better and then move to the next patient – someone who genuinely cares about you. Someone who will fight for you, help you where you need it, and sometimes, even be with you when you don't want them, but when you need them.

I think the world needs more people who are willing to fight to be beside the ones they care for, not a world where pity is what leads relationships, but trust, affection, and a basis that, yeah, I might mess up, but as long as I look to the future with those I care about, maybe a mistake is okay.

CHAPTER 3

The FBT Bus Isn't for Everyone

By Elissa Booth

It's been a wild road trip, but our final destination is much better than our starting point. I asked our daughter if it would be okay for me to share our journey. She hesitated, worried that people would identify her, worried she'd have to read it and that would bring back difficult memories, and worried, I'm sure, about many things. So I told her what I envisioned as the overall message of our passage – "FBT (family-based treatment) is NOT for everyone" – and she instantly fired up. "Yes! Mum, you have to write it. People need to know FBT can do damage, and there are other ways to recover." So, with our daughter's permission, here is our road to recovery.

Where Our Journey Has Led Us

I'll begin at the end – where our travels have led us:

- Our daughter is in strong recovery and living a full life. She's attending high school, doing well academically, playing community basketball, working part-time, coaching Little Athletics, enjoying overseas family vacations, and eating like a typical teenager.
- Our family has gone through a lot of change. I took a year of work leave to focus on being a carer. My husband and I redesigned how we parent and communicate. We set firm boundaries for other family members during recovery.

Things aren't perfect (they never will be). The road to recovery at times felt like an endless expedition, with no compass and cavernous potholes. FBT is a family-based approach to eating disorder (ED) treatment, specifically for persons under the age of 18 years. FBT works for some, but it didn't work for us. So, we hopped off the FBT Bus, chartered our own vehicle, and mapped our own route. I will share some of our "road stops" along the way.

Our daughter gave me the green light to share our trip and drew her boundary to not read it for her own self-care (I'm proud of her for doing so). Part of my self-care has been to find moments to laugh about. So, at the end of each checkpoint, I will tell a story (which you may/may not find funny), because I needed to laugh a little as I looked out the rear-view mirror of our journey.

Road Stop #1: "No Fuel in the Tank"

Our daughter had just turned 13 when we realised something was wrong. Looking back, she had struggled for a couple of years with disordered eating, but it developed into what is clinically considered an eating disorder as she entered Year 8 of high school – atypical anorexia. At this point, she became rapidly unwell – within one to two months.

Our first challenge was getting our daughter medical care. This was for two reasons:

- First, our daughter had "anosognosia". Anosognosia is a medical condition in which someone who is unwell does not think they are unwell. It's not specific to ED, and the person is not intentionally "denying" or "trying to hide" their illness – they truly do not believe they are unwell. Our daughter thought she was fine, everyone else was being ridiculous, and we should just leave her alone.

- Second, our GP was ignorant about ED. Our daughter recognised she was running on empty and tired a lot, but believed it was due to iron deficiency. So I convinced her to go to the GP for an iron test. Meanwhile, I called the GP in advance to advise that I suspected an ED. I was deflated when the GP dismissed my concern, suggested our daughter's heart rate below 50 beats per minute (bpm) was fine since she was an athlete, and sent us back out onto the street.

Unfortunately, this experience reinforced our daughter's belief that she was fine and shifted her recovery into reverse gear. It took another month for our daughter to become so unwell that she ran out of fuel to keep driving down her lane, and I was able to grab the steering wheel and take the off-ramp to the hospital.

A Carer's Takeaway – Road Stop #1:

- Many people with ED don't "look" like they have an eating disorder.
- Trust your gut – if you think your loved one is unwell, they likely are. The medical community is often ignorant about ED.
- Do whatever you need to in order to get help.

ROADSIDE REST STOP

"Tag, You're It!"

At the beginning, our daughter was hyper-aware of clothing sizes. So, I decided it might be helpful to remove this daily stressor by cutting the size tags out of her clothing. Sounds good, until you find yourself in a store dressing room, smuggling in your daughter's clothes to try on (requiring Cirque du Soleil contortionist flexibility because you're nowhere near her size)… in an effort to figure out what size her garments are, to replenish them. And then, your daughter busts you at home for swapping her clothes.

HA! … Yes, our daughter is incredibly PERCEPTIVE.

Road Stop #2: "The FBT Bus Rolls In"

Our local children's hospital has an ED ward, so they were more knowledgeable than our GP. After five hours in the emergency waiting room (where our daughter lobbied repeatedly to leave), they took our daughter's heart rate – and immediately transported her to the "Resuscitate Room". This was because, although to many she seemed fine (including the GP), her resting heart rate had dropped to a terrifying 35bpm. For those who don't know, a heart rate below 50 is a criterion for eating disorder admission in most Australian states/territories; 35bpm is incredibly dangerous – it meant her engine could fail at any point.

They admitted our daughter to the ED ward for two weeks. During this time, she received critical medical support (24/7 heart rate monitoring, medication to prevent life-threatening refeeding syndrome, supervised meals, etc.), but no mental health support. A hospital ED team member briefed my husband and me on FBT in a 20-minute driving lesson in the hallway and told us we would receive outpatient FBT support via CYMHS (Child and Youth Mental Health Services).

The ED team member (who had good intentions) told us repeatedly, "FBT is the 'gold standard'. It's the only clinically proven ED treatment for youth. You're educated, capable adults. You just have to stick to the path – no matter what." Essentially, hop on the FBT Bus, don't look out the windows or pay attention to the deafening screams from the back seat, just keep your eyes on the road and drive top speed ahead. So, with our roadmap in hand, we began FBT at home.

A Carer's Takeaway – Road Stop #2:
- Medical intervention is at times essential and lifesaving.
- The medical community means well but often follows a "one-size-fits-all" approach.

ROADSIDE REST STOP

"When One Door Closes, Another Door Opens."

When we started FBT at home, our daughter's compulsion to exercise was intense. One evening, she started towards the front door to "go for a run". I shifted into gear and did what the FBT books instructed – I grabbed a blanket, wrapped it around her, and tried to stop her. We ended up on the floor, with lots of colourful words directed my way. My husband and I thought, "It worked! We stopped her from heading out the front door!" Twenty minutes later, she slipped out the back door, hopped over our eight-foot fence, and was on her run.

HA! ... Yes, our daughter is incredibly DETERMINED.

Road Stop #3: "The FBT Bus Breaks Down"

Three days after the first hospital admission, we were back at the hospital for another two weeks. Two weeks later, we were back for a third admission. The "FBT travel plan" turned our home into an obstacle course filled with medical sinkholes, trust stop signs, and communication road closures. Our daughter (and our family) was miles worse, physically and mentally. At this point on the motorway, the FBT Bus had an epic four-tyre blowout and was fully engulfed in flames.

The devastation we felt at that time is now hard to describe with words. It felt like being broken down in the desert, with no water, no tow truck, and no mobile service to dial 000. It was then we realised the hospital and CYMHS were essential for medical safety, but that we needed a route to recovery other than FBT that would work for our family. I also admitted that I couldn't work as well as be the carer-parent our daughter needed (I wasn't succeeding at either, and running on fumes myself), so I took a year-long leave of absence from work to focus on her recovery and our family.

A Carer's Takeaway – Road Stop #3:
- FBT's success rate is only ~50%.
- FBT can severely damage trust between you and your loved one.
- FBT can cause enduring PTSD (for them and you).

ROADSIDE REST STOP

"Oh, You Meant 'Weigh-in' … Not 'Bring-in' Weights?"
We went weekly to CYMHS for FBT support. This entailed our daughter getting her obs checked (weight, heart rate, etc.)

and a family counselling session. One day after a CYMHS appointment, I was in the living room and heard a loud "thud, thud" sound from the floor above (which was our daughter's bedroom). Later that day, I went into her room to do some laundry. Under the pile of clothes she had worn to the CYMHS appointment, I found two barbell weights strung through her pants belt.

HA! … Yes, our daughter is incredibly SMART.

Road Stop #4: "Finding a Travel Convoy"

While it was clear that FBT wouldn't work for us, we had no idea which road to turn down. However, two things were clear: 1) we needed to jump into the driver's seat and start exploring the landscape, and 2) we needed our daughter to see us as her "co-pilot" on the journey, not the "police". Building knowledge and rebuilding trust were essential.

I read every book about ED that I could find. Eating Disorders Families Australia (EDFA) was also an incredible roadside service station, filled with travel supplies and a safe convoy of fellow travellers. Among many things, EDFA offered:

- Expert webinars (both live and an archive of past recordings) from world-class leaders in ED detailing different treatments and support methods.
- Links to websites that offered practical trainings and recommendations.
- A network of carers who offered their experience, resources, compassion, and understanding.

- Weekly facilitated support groups for carers and their families.

At this segment of our trip, I discovered several new road-worthy tools:

- EFFT (Emotion Focused Family Therapy) – which helped me understand how to reframe my communication with our daughter, so that she'd talk to me.
- TBT-S (Temperament-Based Therapy with Supports) – which empowers your loved one to use their natural traits and strengths for recovery.
- Cognitive Behavioural Therapy – which teaches that changing thought patterns affects how we feel and act.
- "Scaffolding" – which identifies what brings your loved one joy and helps them build it into their lives, because they need to have something to recover for.
- "Walking alongside your loved one, at their pace" – which acknowledges that while we want our loved one to fast-track to wellness, they must walk the recovery road at the pace they are ready to travel.

We started to test-drive elements of different treatment approaches on our own. If it worked, we kept doing it. If it didn't work, we stopped. One of these approaches that I didn't list above was hypnotherapy for ED. I had watched a webinar via EDFA on this treatment approach and found someone in our area who offered it.

The local ED hypnotherapist had "lived ED experience", which was huge! She explained that she did both hypnotherapy and counselling sessions. (She also did hypnotherapy for gut health at a local clinic, which, if you aren't aware, is 80% effective for gut health.) So, I asked our daughter if she'd be willing to try it. By this time, our daughter was road-weary of medical practitioners kicking the tyres, and she hated talking about feelings. She asked to think about it. After about a month, I gently brought it up again, and our daughter agreed to try it.

A Carer's Takeaway – Road Stop #4:

- Recovery is possible via many different pathways.
- ED is a psycho-metabolic illness. It rewires neural pathways and changes body chemistry. Thus, both physiological and mental aspects need addressing.
- Find your own path and convoy – research, network, ask questions, listen.

ROADSIDE REST STOP

"1970s Multi-colour Polyester is the New Black."

A hospital ED ward can be very disheartening. Moments of joy are rare, but essential. So, with every admission, I brought in one of our dogs to make the rounds to whoever wanted a furry cuddle. One day, I decided to rev it up a gear. I swung by the thrift shop and dressed our girl pup in full *Kath & Kim* bling – colourful tutu onesie, plastic-flower headband, necklaces … and I wore the 1970s polyester leisure jacket my daughter had threatened I could never wear in public with her. It was a fabulous multi-coloured polyester catwalk (well, dogwalk) through the ward. My daughter laughed incredibly hard that day, which was a gift.

HA! … Yes, our daughter has an amazing SPIRIT.

Road Stop #5: "Switching to a Jeep and Off-Roading"

Our first test-drive with the Eating Disorder Hypnotherapist was unlike any road we had travelled. Her office was filled with plants, art, sunlight, and a tiny puppy who sat in our laps. She explained to our daughter what hypnotherapy was, that it was our daughter's choice whether to do it, and that she would share things they spoke about with me/husband only if our daughter agreed (of course, unless harm/self-harm was discussed). Within 20 minutes, our daughter connected with the hypnotherapist so well that I stepped out of the room so they could talk without me. As our daughter later explained, "Mum, she had an eating disorder. She gets it." We left the FBT Bus in the rear-view mirror and were now in an open-air jeep with fresh air and sunlight streaming in.

Over the course of a year or so, sessions with the hypnotherapist (90% counselling, 10% hypnotherapy) helped us unlock life. I say "life" because we talked very little about what our daughter ate. The hypnotherapist understood that medical stability was critical (which we supported via other medical resources). She focused on helping our daughter and our family unpack the luggage in the boot – to help her understand her thoughts that were driving her feelings and leading her to control her food (aspects of cognitive behavioural therapy).

On a parallel service road, our daughter missed aspects of her "old life". So we supported her to consciously start re-engaging in the things that brought her joy (and equally importantly, to stop doing the things that didn't).

This meant:

- Starting back at school, one class/one day at a time. As her health improved, she added more classes – eating lunch with me outside school, in the car.

- Re-introducing exercise, safely. Every day we picked a new park to discover. We would often take her snack to eat while we walked (easier for her versus sitting at a table). In winter, we'd go to a museum to walk.
- Rediscovering her love of sport. My husband and I were clueless that elite sport had become more pressure than fun for her. She decided she wanted to restart it, but only at the community sports level.

As a family, we stopped putting focus on "achievements" and "doing what's expected" and instead focused on "enjoyment" and "giving it a go". This was incredibly hard after 15 or so years of parenting (plus being raised to value these things). Caring for our daughter also meant telling extended family that they could not see our daughter if they could not follow some basic road rules on what to say/not say or do/not do. This wasn't easy either – but I was fiercely uncompromising on this, as it was essential for our daughter's recovery.

As a carer, I also felt an internal drive to help make a difference for other families. National funding for eating disorders was extremely limited. I discovered "Citizens' Petitions", where everyday citizens can submit a petition to Canberra, and the Parliament would assign it to a minister to respond. Fortunately, our local Federal MP agreed to sponsor my petition in Canberra, and several organisations (EDFA, Butterfly Foundation) and public individuals agreed to help spread the word. We raised over 7000 signatures and helped drive awareness and cross-party discussion in Parliament. Later that year, due to the efforts of many people and organisations, an additional $40 million was dedicated from the national budget for ED education and support.

At the beginning of our daughter's journey, I let our daughter know that I had an eating disorder when I was younger. The 2000 Human Genome Project discovered that ED is genetic. Said another way, genetics is the #1 risk factor for developing an eating disorder. If it runs in your family, it doesn't mean it'll manifest, but you're at a much higher risk. ED ran in both my and my husband's families. It was important that our daughter knew that genetics played a key role in her illness, and to remove any perception of shame.

Carer's Takeaway – Road Stop #5:
The #1 risk factor for developing an eating disorder is genetics. So let go of the shame!

- It's exhausting and terrifying to chart your own path, but listen to your loved ones and your gut to find it.
- Talk to your mate (spouse, bestie, family, etc) about skill sets and how to best carve out who does what to support your loved one, each other, and your family.

ROADSIDE REST STOP
"Where's that ED-Recovery Magical Time Portal?"
In one session with the hypnotherapist, our daughter stated sheepishly, "It's taken me a couple of years to recover, but Mum did it in nine months." I was very confused. Our daughter explained her belief that I took a year off from university and returned recovered. "Mum, you went into some kind of magical time portal, and nine months later came out recovered." We all had a good laugh together. I explained to our daughter that it took me about ten years

to fully recover. Instead of thinking she was "not as strong as Mum", she should realise that she has "battled like a warrior, even stronger than Mum".

HA! … Yes, our daughter is incredibly STRONG.

The Final Destination: "New Wheels – Ready for Road Trips"

Looking back – on both my ED and our daughter's ED – it's been both horrific and a blessing. I wouldn't wish an eating disorder on anyone. However, I acknowledge that it prevented my life from taking a path that was not right for me. It helped our daughter develop the courage to pursue her dreams rather than others' expectations, and it also helped our family improve our relationships.

I (and our daughter) also believe that ED is not something "to be kicked out" of our brain and body. We've had medical practitioners tell us this. ED is part of who we are and part of our life journey. It has made us more self-aware … and undeniably, fiercely stronger.

Our journey has had many dark nights with broken headlights, running on fumes, driving in reverse, and careering off the side of the road, only to low gear our way back up embankments. However, by trusting our "internal gut compass" on what was right for our daughter and our family, we found our recovery path. I hope you find your compass, your vehicle, your convoy, and your designated driver when you need a break.

Sending you love, light, and strength for the journey ahead.

CHAPTER 4

Believe

By Leah Ward

Sparkling, quite literally, she is sparkling.

Dressed in a dazzling white gown, physically and mentally happy and living in a world filled with love and joy, my daughter fought so hard to reach this moment. It was not lost on her. It was certainly not lost on me. This was her engagement party, but for me, it was also a joyful celebration of her genuine engagement in life.

Healthy again, happy again, and standing proudly, central in a room full of beloved friends and family with her fiancé by her side. All here to celebrate their recent engagement, all knowing how significant this is after a life challenge that few can truly understand.

With a grateful tremble in her voice, Olivia, now smiling and confident, delivers a speech of love and thanks to the room …

"My 17-year-old self would never have believed this could be possible."

As her primary carer, I had so many moments when it also seemed like an impossibility to me. But it's true – my daughter found a way to believe in her own ability to be well AND genuinely happy. To challenge her negative mind space AND gradually do the work needed to be physically and mentally strong. It was such an inconceivably tough journey, one that I'm assuming many readers who are also carers would be familiar with.

For those on the outside, it's not easy to really understand the frightening depths of the journey Olivia has been on. The tough journey we have all been on in supporting her towards wellness. It's not easy to understand the fear, the exhaustion, the relentless effort, the emotional stretch, the resilience we needed, that she needed in order to be well today.

I didn't count how many hospital admissions she had or how many trips to the emergency department. I didn't count the ambulances, sleepless nights, or appointments with GPs, psychiatrists, dieticians, psychologists, and the range of other experts that helped us to navigate a way forward when it felt like we were swimming through mud. I know one thing; it was all-consuming, and being the primary carer was the toughest thing I have ever needed to do in my life.

Olivia has been recovered now for over three years, but it still triggers grief and sadness for me, a quiet fear of her eating disorder returning, whilst also pinching myself that her life is so much brighter now. I know we are fortunate that Olivia is well, and our life has returned to "normal", whatever that really is. What I do know is that I do not live in fear the same way that I did. I know that Olivia is not afraid of food and its consequences. I know that Olivia deeply accepts that nutrition is strength and it brings breadth to life. She learnt to trust in and focus on making her life bigger than her eating disorder. I had to have faith in some of the choices she made, and we needed to let her have room to "fall" so she could figure out her own way through. When someone with anorexia nervosa falls over, it is terrifying. It is medically dangerous; it's life-threatening; it's distrustful. It's also counterintuitive to the belief I was trying to hold. There was only one way to get through this, and for me, that was to believe she could be well again … and keep believing in this every single day. I also needed to keep believing this for Olivia, as she often was unable to find that belief for herself.

So, what is it to believe?

Usually, believing in something requires evidence and facts to support it. Believing usually occurs when you have so much certainty, well-considered credence, and faith. Belief provides direction, safety, and predictability. In eating disorders, there is only one thing that is certain: it's the opposite of all of this. The juxtaposition is screamingly loud.

What got me through was believing that Olivia's survival and a bright future were actually achievable. I would tell her daily that I knew she could do this and that I believed that good health was possible. It was not always received well; her eating disorder screamed back at me, attacking my optimism along with my three meals and three snacks. My belief was not always optimism; it was a fearful, silent hope often dressed up in the best way tolerable for each difficult moment.

Deep down, I can tell you that believing her recovery was possible was something I needed to convince myself of as well. It was too painful to believe anything different, as it felt like giving up. I knew that the real work sat with her; all I could do was help provide the environment that best allowed her to start believing in herself again. Olivia needed to find value within herself in order to challenge the hurricane of noise in her mind and the physical rejection of nutrition. I had to have faith that my belief in her recovery would also help her believe it was possible. It was such a strong mantra for me (and, I hoped, for us) that I even had two bar bracelets with the word "BELIEVE" engraved on them, so we could both wear them as a constant reminder of what we needed to hold on to. This helped give me faith that we would find a way through. Olivia needed to see me wearing it too; it was on my wrist through every dark moment. The BELIEVE bracelet was somehow grounding.

Throughout Olivia's illness, some moments stand out as turning points. They were often among the lowest and most frightening, and it was only with some reflection, when my nervous system had time to calm down, that I could see them clearly. The highly charged emotional state you experience as a carer is exhausting and blinding. Whilst Olivia's nervous system and unwell body and mind were attacking her and threatening her life, mine was also on the highest alert, in a state of fight, flight, or freeze. When I think back to moments that marked some of the scariest events, I can still feel them in my tightening skin, my elevated heart rate, and my tense shoulders. I can now breathe through these feelings, but at the time, as a carer, this felt almost impossible.

When Olivia was sick, we went through the typical start-up journey of family-based therapy (FBT), delivered in textbook fashion, which was considered the "gold standard". For us, it was an absolute failure and a trigger to an incredibly heightened risk of self-harm, extreme agitation, and depression. Poor mental health had already been a challenge for Olivia prior to her eating disorder taking hold. With FBT, the care of her mental health seemed to be fully withdrawn. Something that she was extremely distressed by, and something I needed to listen to. I did not disagree that Olivia needed adequate, regular nutrition to bring her body back into a safe metabolic state where it could function and heal. Still, the expected delivery seemed to lack compassion. As a family, we were in a world of pain, trying to understand and navigate this new medical and psychological hell we were in. What I felt it lacked was a focus on her as an individual – not just the calories – and I questioned the demeaning methods employed to ensure the calories were delivered.

Where did Olivia sit in the middle of all of this? Being taught to insist on specific caloric amounts in each meal or snack, whilst very little attention seemed to be paid to who she was and what her mind was harassing her with. There isn't one mould for all eating disorder patients. I knew my daughter needed more, and she was begging for this. It wasn't always through clear and articulate, calm language; it was in her loud, explosive, and heartbreaking pain and distress. There had to be a better way, and I refuse to believe that all people with anorexia nervosa are explicitly the same. Olivia was the individual trapped in the middle of this illness, and she needed to be seen, heard, and validated before any food would comfortably pass by her lips.

But how to validate her extremely loud thoughts when they seem so wrong, so irrational, and so oppositional to me? This was never easy, and to this day, I still find that the most challenging part. What I needed to do (and what I did my best to do) was pay attention to and validate her pain. Her pain was phenomenal. Her pain was real. It was all-consuming, and until that was truly seen and explored, how could she even consume what she needed through nutrition to survive? Olivia was the person trapped in this eating disorder, and separating it as another being was demeaning to her. It was her. She was it.

Securing the support she needed to find herself again, even amid the illness, had to be a priority. In addition to the manualised FBT program, I sought help separately and worked on building my strength and compassion to face the tidal wave that engulfed us. External counselling (which was not included in the FBT guidelines) was a priority for us. I found a psychologist who had an emotional support dog for Olivia. I joined the EDFA to seek support for my journey as a carer, to build my knowledge and find new angles. It was a gradual, constant process. I had my daughter on just about every waitlist in Melbourne because the system made it difficult. I hassled receptionists and followed up on every given opportunity. I read books and leaned on new friends who were in this, too.

I refused to just let the eating disorder take her, which meant losing sleep, compromising my job, neglecting my family, not getting the lawn mowed, not having a personal relationship, and getting behind on other life admin. Olivia needed to be front and centre. Being a single parent meant that I could not stop working, and to be honest, I still do not know how I did this. I think I lived on very little sleep for years, and my cortisol levels were no doubt through the roof, but somehow, we survived.

After a couple of years of battling Olivia's illness from so many angles and new directions (post the difficult FBT starting point), we met an amazing eating disorder educator. She had genuine insight into the psyche of many with this illness, gained through decades of lived experience as a carer and educator. Someone I will always be incredibly grateful to for all that she brought to our lives. This work was coupled with all the other medical layers of care Olivia had in place, and it helped us find a new approach focused on her inner experience of the world. Olivia started to really feel seen and understood whilst being entrusted with specific work that peeled back her heavily layered onion. I also thought that I was given the support to step back and allow Olivia the room to work through her negative headspace and start making some decisions for herself. I had been living in so much fear for so long, and this support helped me to breathe a little, although trusting it was not instinctive.

With new encouragement, we went through the tough, exhaustive, and expensive process to explore Olivia's potential neurodivergence. With this eventual diagnosis and the relief it gave Olivia, she started to build some confidence in trusting her body and that she could safely give it the nutrition it was begging for. Her fears of overindulgence were tackled and supported as she found balance again. It took time and had many ups and downs, but gradually, Olivia could see her innate value and genuinely decided that she was worth fighting for. This didn't come without the depths of health risk as her eating disorder gripped tightly, what felt like unreasonable hospital discharges, family stress and grief, tangled and messy. Things seemed to get a lot worse before they got better. I kept believing that her recovery was possible but held the strong position that the work and outcomes were up to my daughter. She needed to believe in it, too. She needed to find a reason to believe it.

As Olivia explored what her neurodivergence diagnosis meant for her, there was an avalanche of new emotions. Relief that she no longer believed that she was hopeless, wrong, or took up too much space. I was able to work on reducing environmental stress to make the hard nutritional work more bearable (like dimmer lights, a quieter home, comfortable clothing, fidget toys, and more involvement in scheduling). Olivia started to receive support more heavily directed towards her neurodivergent mental health needs and trauma as she stepped into taking responsibility for her physical health. It was amazing to watch this blossom and evolve, to slowly feel my shoulders drop, even if only a little. I could start to breathe again.

Olivia does not recall a single moment when she decided to recover. Aiming for a perfect recovery through tasks and challenges made things tougher for Olivia and her neural wiring. It was the focus on making other elements of life far more important. She gradually sought personal evidence that the hard work and discomfort (often extreme) were worth it for the new hobby, activity, friend, or work she wanted to explore. Olivia began living her life without feeling ashamed of how she experienced it. Previously, in the more challenging times, her eating disorder would be her fallback position as other things in her life were not big enough to pull her forward and keep her there. Stepping out of the recovery bubble and into life brought reason and something more exciting to focus on. Things that rewarded Olivia opened her world, and they also needed her well-fuelled energy. Olivia reflects on psychiatric inpatient and FBT being so "cookie-cutter", and her neurodivergent brain needed to seek its own evidence to make the uncomfortable release of eating disorder habits possible.

I believe Olivia started to see glimpses of her sparkle, her value, and life's possibilities. After not being able to drive for some time, Olivia wanted to spend the money she had previously saved to buy a car. By this time, Olivia was 21, and she also wanted to return to work at a local supermarket. All of this required me to have faith and believe that she would be able to manage her recovery whilst adding these "risks" into the mix. But were they risks, or were they opportunities to live, to find value and purpose again? It most definitely turned out to be the latter, and I'm so grateful that she pushed me to trust her. I found this time so hard, as the progress she was making could easily have been lost.

Clearly, it was her time. Olivia not only started driving again, enjoying some independence, but also felt a great sense of purpose in the routine of work and in the freedom of decision-making. This leap of faith also led Olivia to meet her future fiancé, and with so many wonderful elements in her life, the many reasons to be well were there awaiting her grasp. It was time to really get on with living and a full recovery. We gratefully witnessed a constant but slow path forward when these things all fell into place. Olivia gradually grew increasingly positive about the benefits of being well, and her determination to not return to the illness became bigger than the eating disorder itself.

After recovery, there was a moment that really sticks with me, and writing about it still brings tears of love and gratitude to my eyes. It was about 18 months after Olivia really started to embrace recovery that she came to me one day and told me that she was "sorry that she could not see it". Olivia had found an old phone that she had with her during her years of illness, and it accompanied her in many hospital stays. Her eating disorder had convinced her she was not thin, was not sick, and was not in danger. What I was seeing – and the evidence the selfie images on her phone showed – was a very different story.

Olivia charged up her old phone and, with healthy eyes and mind, now looked through the old, frightening photos. What was reflected at her was a very different person from what her memory had held, and possibly for the first time, Olivia saw how dangerously sick she really was. Previously, I was wrong; it was every doctor who was wrong. She didn't believe what we were saying to her at that time, but here she was now, thanking me for believing in her, for holding hope, and for not giving up on her.

After having so much thrown at me while Olivia was sick, receiving this gratitude and genuine visibility was such a powerful and emotional moment. One I had struggled to believe would ever be possible. It was so bonding and showed me that love holds strong and relationship strength can be rebuilt when all seems lost.

When I was asked to write this chapter, the first person I needed to speak to about it was my brave daughter.

Her beautiful response has been so motivating, and I hope that it helps others to see that the awful feelings of being ill can pass. Her words to me were immediate: "Mum, I'm not ashamed of being sick. You should tell the story." This really sat with me and made me reflect on how heartbreaking shame can be.

When my daughter was sick, shame sat heavily, thick and sticky like hot tar. It had her glued to the heater vent, wrapped in a blanket to keep her drained body warm. It led her to withdraw from everyone and everything that gave her joy. It had been yelling ongoing abuse at her, not audible to me, but visible in how she carried her stressed body. Shame made her sick and kept her ill. It deserved no place in my daughter. She had no reason to be ashamed. She did not deserve the full-scale abuse this illness threw at her. It didn't belong in our home. It didn't deserve to follow her to school, to the hospital, to all of her appointments, and shame certainly did not have a right to sit next to her at our dinner table. But there it was, taking the space where love belonged. Thick like hot tar. It must have felt impossible to shed.

Did believing that Olivia could be well and that she deserved a full life, filled with adventure, good health, and dreams, actually make any difference? I know believing isn't a magic pill – if only there were one. I do know that deeply and genuinely believing that Olivia could be well once more actually kept me going. I also believe that, in some way, it helped her keep going when her body was close to giving up.

To my daughter, Olivia, I am so proud of you and so thankful that you let me in, in whatever way was possible at the time. I will never forget the phenomenal strength you have shown. I will never stop being immensely grateful that you found your own way through, and you have gone on to let your colours shine.

To the carers, I see you and feel your pain. Each eating disorder journey is different and does not benefit from comparison. All I can wish for you is that you can keep the strength and keep believing that a life of wellness is possible. What it looks like and how you get there will be your story to write. I hope our journey, in some way, helps to give you strength during the most impossibly difficult time in your life.

Please keep believing. They really need you to.

CHAPTER 5

My Gut Told Me So

By Teresa Orth

Acknowledgement

This is my story as a mum who cared for my daughter, who had an eating disorder. I have so much respect for her and the tough fight that she kept on fighting to get to recovery. I am so very proud of my daughter. I feel honoured to be her mum. I also feel honoured that she allows me to share my side of her illness.

To all parents and carers who are supporting a loved one with an eating disorder, I see you, and I know how tough it is to care for someone you love who has this illness. May this book keep hope alive for you.

* * *

As a mum, I just knew something wasn't right with my daughter. For almost two years, my gut kept telling me that what I was seeing wasn't just normal teenage behaviour. I always put it down to the change of hormones and growing through the teenage years. But when I spoke with other parents about their teenagers, I always felt different. Emotions seemed more intense in my daughter. She was constantly moving, always restless. Long showers with loud music. Cooking endless snacks and so enthusiastic about feeding everyone, family and friends. There were signs, but I didn't yet know how to read them. I now know the loud music was to cover up the constant exercise and purging. The cooking was to cover up the fact that she was not eating.

We're a family of four. My husband and I have a daughter and a son. We had a busy, normal family life – work, school, sports for the kids. When our daughter was 14 and our son was 11, we had not had a holiday for two years. We planned a family trip to Tasmania – a break we all needed. My daughter, the perfectionist that she is, insisted on bringing her schoolwork. This gave me bad vibes. She would not allow herself a total break from her routine. During this holiday, we stayed together in hotels and had to share bathrooms for the first time in a while. This is when I saw physical signs. There were bruises on her spine. I asked her what happened. "Don't worry, Mum. I'm all good, just bumped myself." In that moment, I felt my inklings were correct. Something was very wrong with my daughter.

I have always been someone who thinks things through. I like to solve problems, but do not like to be rushed. I like to think and analyse. Often, I overthink things, but I have found that when I listen to my instincts and think them through, I am generally correct. My daughter is also an overthinker. She is still learning, growing, and getting to know herself better. She is so strong-willed and wants to be independent. This is one of the things I love about her. When we returned home from our holiday, I knew I had to get my daughter to a doctor.

I could not just tell her what to do. There had to be a reason other than my suspicions. I used the excuse of renewing a script for her. When we saw our GP, she knew something wasn't right. The GP checked her vitals and chatted with her. My daughter complained of having a sore tummy. She told the doctor she would get tummy pains and did not feel like eating. I had been seeing this doctor for a few years. She knew me well. This GP was the right fit for our family. I know now that this was so important for us. Our GP gave us a referral to a paediatric gastroenterologist. We were lucky to get an appointment within two weeks. The GP recommended that both my husband and I attend this appointment. I'm thankful this was her advice to us. I was so relieved to have been able to get my daughter to the doctor.

In the days leading up to the appointment, my daughter was barely eating. She was so critically unwell. Our house was under a lot of stress at this time. Both my husband and I could see that our daughter needed to eat. Our daughter kept yelling at us, telling us her tummy was too sore to eat. I couldn't sleep well because I was so worried about her. In these two weeks, it was the first time I had food thrown in my face – so much heightened emotion. I could sense there was something she was going through that none of us understood. I was desperate to get her to this specialist.

Finally, it was time to see the specialist. Both my husband and I attended. I had taken the day off work, and my daughter had the day off school. My husband worked in the morning and met us at the specialist's rooms. That same afternoon, my daughter was admitted to hospital. Her blood sugar levels were dangerously low. She was hypothermic. Her heart was at risk. In hospital, my daughter had to have a feeding tube. A nasogastric (NG) tube. I was in total shock. I felt sick. I have lots of memories with NG tubes. My daughter was a premmie baby and spent the first five weeks of her life in hospital.

I felt so much guilt, kept questioning myself and my actions as a mum over the past weeks and months. My daughter was admitted to hospital for an eating disorder. Eating disorder, why? I always saw her eating. How did this happen? How did I miss this? This is when I first heard, "Your daughter has anorexia nervosa." I heard it, but I didn't understand it. I also didn't want to hear it. I just wanted my daughter to be well again. The nurses and mental health team were kind, compassionate, and knowledgeable. They helped us understand what we were facing. This was not just a phase. It was a serious mental illness. Mental illness! I had no idea that anorexia nervosa was a mental illness.

The hospital admission was the start of our steep learning curve. We were overwhelmed with information: websites to refer to, books to read, and appointments to be made. I felt naïve. Helpless. Looking into my daughter's eyes, I could see she was lost. I would have done anything to bring her back. Somehow, I found a strength I didn't know I had. I kept listening to my instincts and kept staying strong for my daughter. When you are emotionally stressed, you become more vulnerable. Professionals and friends had various views and opinions. Little did they know that their language and actions, or non-actions, were creating a sense of shame, guilt, and blame. I kept away from those who gave me bad vibes. I had to prioritise myself to stay strong and focused for my daughter. I knew this was the only way I might get my daughter back to living life to her fullest.

After ten days in hospital, we were sent home to take care of our daughter. She was medically stable. We were told to take our daughter to the doctor weekly. This also meant weekly blood tests, weekly ECGs, and weekly checks of vitals, including weight, to keep her monitored and ensure she stayed medically stable. When we got home, my husband stayed with her for two weeks while I went to work. When my husband returned to work, we decided that I would stay home with my daughter to care for her. I just knew I could not send my daughter back to school. If my daughter had returned to school, she would have ended up back in the hospital repeatedly. I did not totally understand this illness at this stage. My instincts told me that I had to stay home with her. I did not do any paid work for seven months. I became my daughter's full-time carer.

Having to stop work created another stress in our lives. We were a family with a mortgage and relied on both incomes to maintain our lifestyle as it was. We were lucky we had some savings to help us. It got to the point where we had to ask our bank for assistance. We applied for financial hardship with our financial institution. That was something I thought I would never have to do. My husband and I also discussed selling our home and downsizing to reduce our debt. We were exploring all options to ensure our daughter could get to a healthy life in the time she needed. It is so horrible that a critical illness, a critical mental illness, is so debilitating in so many ways for families trying to get on the road to recovery.

Our daughter's recovery began at home. We were given a meal plan from the hospital. It was the first meal plan, a simple one to help my daughter start eating again. This was a tough time at home for the family – an even tougher time for my daughter. My husband and I didn't really understand what we were dealing with. I believed I just had to do as I was told, follow the rules and do what the doctors and nurses said. Recovery from an eating disorder is a marathon, not a sprint. Every single day was so very challenging to get my daughter to eat. This illness would try to avoid food at all costs. We kept going, pushing through all the heightened emotions. I kept pushing my daughter to take one bite at a time, constantly asking her to take one more bite. Just one more. "It's what your body needs to stay at home and not return to the hospital."

We decided to name the eating disorder. We googled "mean girl names" and chose one that had no association with anyone we knew. It helped to separate the illness from our daughter.

This really worked well for our family. It gave us something to fight.

We stayed engaged with my daughter's school. The deputy principal was incredibly supportive, and would say, "Get well first – then we'll support you back into school." This meant so much to us. It was especially important for my daughter to hear from the school leadership that they would support her and give her time to become well, so she could then return to school.

It took about three months until we had an appointment with a specialist eating disorder team. We saw a psychiatrist first. My daughter had physical, emotional, mental, and behavioural assessments done. A bone density scan revealed that our 14-year-old had the bone density of an 80-year-old.

After our daughter's assessment, we had an appointment with the psychiatrist. It was clearly explained to our daughter that we would take charge of her life. The starvation syndrome was explained to us, and what starvation does to our bodies. It was confronting. A second, stricter meal plan was introduced. Bathroom doors had to remain open. Bedroom doors open. No hiding. No exercising. We were strict with the illness, but gentle with our daughter. Naming the illness helped. This reminded us that the cruel behaviours weren't her – they were the illness.

After the assessments with the psychiatrist, we started family-based therapy (FBT). This was with a social worker who specialised in eating disorders. FBT worked for us. Every day was a battle, not with my daughter, but with the illness. FBT helped us fight as a family. Food was the medicine. My daughter's mental illness saw the food as a weapon. Every bite was a win. We also learned that laughter was medicine. Some days it felt impossible, but when we could laugh, even just briefly, it all felt so much better. FBT was once a week. It created higher distress for my daughter as more specialists were trying to assist her to stay on the path to wellness. I am my child's expert. I have known my child the longest. I know what food she likes and dislikes. I grew to know when the eating disorder was shining most in my child. I will never forget the look in her eyes, glazing over, looking lost; I wanted her to be herself. I fought for my child when she could not fight for herself.

Our son saw it all. We were always honest with him. There was no way of hiding this illness in our home; there was just open, age-appropriate truth. He is naturally a kind, nurturing person. He also helped his sister get to recovery. We did not force or ask him to; he helped when he felt he could. As mentioned previously, eating is so challenging for someone who has an eating disorder. Distraction from food is a good technique we were taught to use – distraction before, during, and after mealtimes. My son, when he could, chose to give his sister plenty to distract her. I remember one time after a meal, he let her dress him up with make-up and a dress. I remember this so well, as there was so much laughter with the whole family. So much laughter from our daughter. It was the first time we had laughed like that in a while.

Once again, I kept getting this inkling that what we were doing was not enough to get her to recovery. FBT helped, but I did not feel it was helping enough. Through perseverance and asking questions, we were accepted into an eating disorder day program. This program was run by a multidisciplinary team, including nurses, social workers, occupational therapists, psychologists, and psychiatrists. All on the same page. All assisting us to fight the illness.

The day program was Monday to Friday, with a 9 a.m. drop-off, a 3 p.m. pick-up, and a half-day on Wednesday. We supplied the food, and it was checked in every morning to ensure the illness could not trick anyone. My daughter was engaged with schoolwork and getting the help she needed.

The day program's routine was intense. The program is meant to be intense, with total focus on getting to recovery one step at a time. As gruelling as it was, it gave me an opportunity to return to some work. It was only for a few hours a day, but it meant I was keeping in touch with my work. I was lucky I had a great boss who supported me. My work colleagues did question me. "How much longer do you need to do this, Teresa? You can't go on like this – you are going to break down yourself." I heard this constantly, from people who meant well, who looked out for me, but they did not understand this mental illness. So complex. I was not giving up. If I gave up on fighting this mental illness that consumed my daughter, I felt that would mean I was giving up on my daughter. Looking back at the juggle, I feel lucky my workplace was so busy. This enabled me to focus on something else – even if it was for a few hours a day. My work was my break away from this gruelling, consuming mental illness known as anorexia nervosa.

As part of this program, my husband and I were required to attend an Emotionally Focused training. This training taught us skills I wish every parent had – how to validate feelings, tolerate distress, and avoid staying in overwhelming emotions. I had to unlearn the "tough it out" mentality from my upbringing. That mindset wasn't going to help our daughter recover.

This education was pivotal. I had to relearn how to handle intense emotion – for my daughter and for myself. At this moment, I really understood that an eating disorder was a mental illness.

Anorexia nervosa is more than just about food. It's about disordered thoughts, actions, and emotions. It's clever. It convinces your child to stay unwell. There is no rational thinking.

It takes over, and it punishes. Punishes the individual with the illness and punishes their loved ones around them.

We had to trust a team of professionals to help guide my daughter out. It took this multidisciplinary team to get to recovery. They gave us tools. They gave my daughter tools, tools I believe she will carry for life.

I now know anorexia nervosa had been ruling our home for about two years before diagnosis. If I had only known the signs to look out for, our journey may have been different.

I felt isolated and ashamed. There's so much stigma around mental illness. People meant well, but their words and actions made me feel guilty. I learned to protect my energy. I stayed close to those who gave me strength and let go of those who made me feel small.

My husband and I learned to use our own strengths to assist our daughter get to recovery. We always ensured we were on the same page, with many phone calls and messages between us. We learned to support each other like never before. Your own emotions get heightened, and this did not help our daughter. We could see how hard it was for her to eat. If we got angry or frustrated, the best thing was to walk away and calm down. My daughter could not be left on her own. If we did, the dog would be well fed. So my husband and I learned to tag team. We would take it in turns to sit with her. I found that my husband was so helpful at dinner time. I was most exhausted from the illness by the end of the day. My husband was exhausted from working, but he would always come home and help. I am so grateful for my husband. It was our teamwork, together, on the same page, that enabled us to get our daughter to recovery.

Through this journey, I have learned to trust my instincts more. I accept and respect others more. Let people be themselves. Embrace all our differences. Don't be afraid to speak up in the way that you are most comfortable with.

The path to recovery became visible to me once I had accepted that this illness was a mental illness. This mental illness changed our family. It forced me to find my strength, and in doing so, I helped my daughter find hers. As a mum, I ensure that I let both my children be themselves. I accept them for who they are. I want them to be confident in who they are in this world. Trust their own instincts. Be accepting of all differences. Be kind and respectful. You never know if anyone is struggling with a mental illness. Don't be afraid to speak up and talk about mental illness. Talking about it and creating awareness reduces isolation; it reduces the shame that is felt by people who have a mental illness or by someone who is caring for someone with a mental illness.

If you're caring for someone with an eating disorder, don't give up. It's hard. It's overwhelming. But your loved one is fighting even harder. Keep showing up. Keep fighting for them until they can fight for themselves.

Mental illness is a health condition that affects thought, mood, and behaviour. It creates distress and can take over a life.

Recovery is possible. But it takes everything you have. I put my needs aside to give my daughter the best chance. I pushed. I rang all the specialists. I kept asking. I kept showing up. I lay next to her in silence, just so she'd feel safe. I would do it all again.

I now have my daughter back.
In helping her find herself,
I found myself, too.

CHAPTER 6

Wrong About Hope

By Katie Bennett-Stenton

If you'd told me, back then, that one day I'd be writing a chapter called "Wrong About Hope", I would have laughed. Not the uplifting kind of laugh that lets light in, but the hollow, brittle laugh of someone convinced hope had packed its bags and left the building.

By nature, I'm deeply and sometimes annoyingly optimistic. A glass-half-full type. The sort of person who believes in grit and perseverance, who thinks most storms eventually pass if you just keep moving. But during those three, maybe four years, though they felt like a decade, that optimism was shredded.

There were suicide attempts. The first was witnessed by her nine-year-old brother, who should have been climbing trees and playing basketball, not absorbing trauma that would shadow him for years. There was self-harm. Hospital stays. Psychiatrists and psychologists like a revolving door. Pregnancy tests in bins. Many nights, when our daughter slipped out into the dark and we scoured the streets, we were frantic with worry. ADHD was finally diagnosed because someone at last listened.

And me: surviving on anti-anxiety medication by day, strong sleeping pills by night. Not thriving. Not "resilient". Running on fumes. Turning up to work with mascara and strategy decks, then collapsing once the laptop shut.

What doesn't show up on a résumé is the soundtrack of those nights, the steady click of the front-door latch as I waited for it to open, the hum of the fridge at 2 a.m., the low-grade, ever-present dread that sat just under my ribcage like static. My husband and I became project managers of crisis: one scanning police logs, the other calling our daughter's friends, both pretending we could out-organise chaos.

And then came another part that no parent could ever imagine. Court appearances followed, tangled in a situation that spiralled completely out of our control. Close family friends, people who knew us deeply, had to seek legal advice and provide sworn statements attesting that we were nurturing, loving parents who adored our children and would never harm them. Child Protection became involved, making an already hellish existence almost unbearable. Our nine-year-old son was interviewed by Child Protection at school without our knowledge, with the deputy principal, whom I knew as a fellow member of the school council, supporting the interview. The process was long, drawn out, and devastatingly unfair, a trauma for us all layered on top of an already broken reality.

It's difficult to describe the peculiar humiliation of that time, how being questioned about your parenting strips you bare, how love becomes evidence, and how quickly dignity drains from a life lived under scrutiny. Feeling nauseous answering the phone to numbers we didn't recognise. What new horror were we now confronted with? We stopped making plans. Even birthdays felt tentative, like temporary permissions to be normal.

If you're reading this in the thick of it, you don't need me to paint the whole picture. You already know the jagged edges.

But here's what matters: I was wrong.

Helen was right.

Our daughter did come through.

The Parents Who Made Me

I grew up with wonderful parents. Both high-school teachers. Both endlessly loving. They were at every single sports game, every debate, every band concert. They clapped the loudest and stayed the longest. Their love was never in question.

They were also structured. Rules, curfews, discipline. Not unkindness, but reliability. It worked for me.

So, of course, I carried that into my own parenting. Home by curfew. Respect the rules. Except when my daughter's eating disorder took hold, those rules didn't just fail; they backfired spectacularly.

I had to unlearn. To parent completely differently. To discover that love sometimes looks like loosening, not tightening.

That was the hardest lesson: the version of me who'd built a life on control had to learn to sit in uncontrollable mess. I, who'd made a career of clarity and strategy, now faced a battlefield where every rule reversed itself overnight. "Don't let her isolate" became "Give her space." "Hold your boundaries" became "Pick your battles." Even my instincts betrayed me.

There were nights I stood outside her door, hand on the handle, rehearsing conversations in my head: if I go in now, will she push me away, or will she see I'm still here? Sometimes I entered anyway, pretending to tidy laundry just to hear her breathing. Hope, in those moments, was microscopic: a sigh, a text, a single bite of toast.

The Career Juggle

At the same time, I was working in marketing and strategy, juggling deadlines and a leadership role. My husband and I both tried to keep the plates spinning, but he managed it with far more steadiness and grace than I did. Looking back, I'd make different choices. Not because ambition is wrong, but because deluding myself that nothing had to give nearly broke me. Careers can recover. Families sometimes don't.

One of the hardest lessons? Accepting that you can't perform at your peak professionally while your home is on fire. And that's not weakness. That's humanity.

Still, I tried. I presented to boards with my phone face-down beside the notes, my heart thudding at every vibration. I left strategy sessions early to answer calls from the police. I wore silk dresses and exhaustion like twin skins. I perfected the art of appearing sort of fine, smiling in meetings, crying in lifts. I learned to mute tears before the Zoom unmuted.

Corporate life has no manual for grief in progress. Colleagues mean well, but their kindness often lands awkwardly, a tilted head, a murmured, "You're so strong." Strength, I discovered, isn't bravery; it's survival dressed for work.

Somewhere amid quarterly targets, the police station, and hospitals, I lost the version of myself that believed performance equalled worth. I began to understand that the truest form of leadership might simply be showing up fractured and honest, modelling imperfection so others could breathe.

Helen, in Fabulous Glasses

And then came a woman who changed everything. Not an angel exactly, but an unlikely saviour in fabulous glasses.

She worked in a public mental-health service. Yes, she had the qualifications. But more importantly, she was a mother who had already walked this road. Her daughter had lived it and emerged. She wasn't theorising. She knew.

Until then, I'd never heard the phrase "lived experience". It sounded flimsy, like something from a cheesy self-help book. But her lived experience was the strongest rope I ever held.

Every week, she gathered parents like me on a 90-minute call. At first, I wondered how on earth I'd spare 90 minutes when I could barely breathe. But those calls became my lifeline.

Sometimes I sat in glass-walled corporate rooms, positioned just so, far enough into the corner that colleagues couldn't see my silent crying as they walked past, the mute button my closest friend. Sometimes I dialled in from home, laptop balanced on knees, tears dripping onto the keyboard. Other parents did the same.

Those calls didn't end the hell. But they made it less lonely.

Over time, the screens became a sanctuary. Faces I'd never met became comrades who understood the shorthand of pain: the lifted eyebrow that meant "Hospital again?", the hollow laugh that meant "Still no progress." We compared notes on medications, treatment plans, and tiny wins: half a meal finished, a smile returned, a day without panic. Hope began as an echo in someone else's voice before it found its way back to mine.

When our official time with her ended, we carried on. I set up a WhatsApp group. I called it "Parents Who Eat". (Humour: the only weapon left when everything else is stripped away.) They laughed. Years later, those parents are among my dearest friends. Just today, we met for my husband's birthday. Survivors. Comrades. Family of choice.

We still text each other during anniversaries of hospital admissions or bad days. We still share recipes, dark jokes, half-jokes about needing cocktails, and photos of kids who once hovered at the edge of life, now grinning with groups of friends. Every message says the same thing beneath the words:

"We made it. And if you're still in the storm, we'll sit with you until it passes."

The Right Support

Not all professionals are equal. Early on, one GP openly admitted she knew nothing about eating disorders and began googling during our consult. We left more terrified than when we'd arrived.

Then we found a GP who truly understood, brilliant, relentless, compassionate. She listened. She fought for referrals. She knew when to push and when to step back. Having the right GP doesn't solve everything, but it changes the trajectory.

And for me personally, my GP became the quiet hero of my survival. She managed my mental-health plans, adjusted my medication, and gave me permission to admit that I was drowning, too. She didn't just treat me as a parent; she treated me as a human being who needed help. Without her, I wouldn't have had the strength to keep going.

Finding those people, the ones who see you and not just the crisis, is pure magic. They hold your hand without taking your agency. They translate clinical language into human words. They say, "I can't fix this, but I can help you hold it." And that, some days, is the difference between collapse and one more step.

Being Wrong About Hope

She used to say: "Your daughter will come through this. There is another side. You have to hold on."

I didn't believe her.

I thought she was wrong.

But she wasn't.

And thank God, it was me who was wrong.

The day I realised that was ordinary. No cinematic crescendo, just a morning when sunlight hit the kitchen tiles and my daughter asked, "What's for dinner?" A real question, not a performance. She ate half. Then laughed at a meme her brother showed her. I stood at the sink and cried silently into the dishwater. Hope doesn't arrive with trumpets; it tiptoes back in disguised as normal life.

The Playbook I Wish I'd Had

For parents in the thick of it, here's what I wish someone had whispered to me. Not the sanitised advice. The real, hard-won truths.

- Unlearn what you know. The rules that worked yesterday may break your child today. Parenting differently isn't failure. It's survival.
- Find your Helens. Professionals are essential. But peers with lived experience are oxygen.
- Enlist the help of clever mates to research. A buddy of mine found the phenomenal GP who specialises in disordered eating. Because she was able to think calmly and strategically. I was not!
- Not all professionals are equal. If your GP doesn't get it, keep looking. The right one is gold. And one of the other parents also found the "hot GP"; she and her daughter are quite happy to go to appointments!
- Humour is medicine. Laugh even when it feels wrong. It's not disrespect. It's oxygen.
- Medication isn't failure. My pills didn't make me weak. They gave me just enough strength to keep showing up.

- Hold onto slivers of normal. Coffee with a friend. Watching terrible TV. A walk. A sneaky gin while out walking the dogs with a buddy. These tiny anchors tether you to the world outside crisis.

- Therapy for siblings matters. Don't assume resilience. My son's school psychologist helped him process what was happening, and his teachers quietly offered extra support. Siblings need their own safe spaces.

- Set emotional boundaries. If someone (even a grandparent) tries to lean on you for their own processing, stop them. You cannot be their therapist. Tell them politely but firmly: get your support elsewhere. Your energy is for your child.

- Be specific when asking for help. People want to help but don't know how. For us, the greatest gifts were friends taking our son out for fun or dropping meals at the door. Practical help was a godsend.

- Name the enemy. Sometimes the only words that help are the bluntest: "F*ck eating disorders." Say it out loud if you need to. It reminds you that this is not your child you're fighting; it's the illness.

- Document the absurd. One day, the things that made you cry may make you laugh. Our WhatsApp thread is proof.

- Ask again. And again. Systems are patchy. Referrals fall through. Keep going. Persistence matters.

- Borrow hope. When you can't carry it, let someone else carry it for you.

- You will believe it's hopeless. You will be wrong.

And one more that took me years to learn: forgive yourself daily. There is no perfect response, no flawless decision. Some nights you will lose your temper or forget to eat, wish for escape, or have wine for dinner. That doesn't make you a bad parent; it makes you human in impossible circumstances.

Why I Write This

Our daughter is doing better than she ever has. She has found her people. She has matured. She is stronger. She (mostly) eats well.

Sometimes she talks about her ADHD medication reducing her appetite and how she doesn't feel like eating, but before she was unwell, she would never have talked about it at all. The fact that she can now speak openly is an extraordinary progress.

Recovery isn't a straight line; it's a spiral staircase. There are dips, yes, but each circle rises a little higher. There are mornings when she hums while making coffee, and I catch myself thinking: "Remember this sound." There are nights when she hugs me unexpectedly, fierce and unguarded, and I realise we are both relearning safety.

When those moments come, we have calm conversations about fuelling the things she loves, her passions, her friendships, her life. I've learned how to be ballast without panic, and she's learned how to let us in. That alone is a miracle.

People sometimes ask if I'm grateful for the experience. I'm not grateful. But I am changed. I know now that hope isn't a destination; it's a daily practice, a quiet discipline, a muscle that rebuilds itself through ordinary acts of love. And I'm hell-bent on making it less cr*p for those who follow. Some good has to come out of the experience; I won't allow it to be any other way.

I can't overstate the difference between where we were and where we are now. For a long time, I was certain my girl wouldn't come through. And there were nights when I wasn't sure our family would either. But we did. She did.

And this is what I want to leave you with: your child, your sibling, your partner, the person you're supporting, can thrive, too. With time, with the right help, and with your ongoing love, they can find a life beyond this illness that you may not be able to imagine right now.

If you're standing in the ruins wondering who you've become, know this: there will be a day when laughter sounds natural again, when dinner isn't a hostage situation, when you can make plans without checking discharge notes first. It will come quietly, but it will come. Hold your nerve. Hold your love. That's the work. And get a damn good therapist.

Hold on. Even if you're sure you can't. Because there is another side, and when you get there, you'll see a version of your loved one and yourself, stronger than you thought possible.

And until then? F*ck eating disorders.

CHAPTER 7

Through the Trenches: A Father's Battle Against Anorexia

By Rohan Michael

We are finally standing in the large ward area after eight hours in the emergency department. Our daughter has been placed in a bed with the hope of her being admitted to receive the treatment she so desperately needs. Without warning, she takes herself down the hospital corridor, running as fast as she can. I quickly take off after her along a fluorescently lit hallway with chequered tiles and pale, nondescript walls. Suddenly, she is out of sight, but I hear footsteps down a stairwell and quickly follow them several levels below. Looking around, there is no sight of her, but I can hear a faint noise of someone trying to open a door. The scraping metal sound gets louder as I approach, and I see my daughter frantically trying to open a door that leads outside the hospital into a dark suburban night. To my relief, it is not opening, but to her, this door is an escape from the reality she is in and the hopelessness, unknowing, and despair of what lies ahead. This door, she believes, is her way out from the unimaginable fear of what she has to face.

This night was long and exhausting for us, every detail etched in my memory. I clearly remember the relief of knowing she had been admitted and was in safe care for the night, but also the awful underlying torment that we had, as her parents, done the unthinkable and refused to take her home, believing this to be the only way we could get her safe, keep her alive, and ensure she started to receive much-needed treatment. She'd had many hospital admissions in the past, but this was the first one as an adult, and we were fast learning that eating disorder treatment looked very different once you crossed over 18 years.

Memories are strange, powerful, and often wonderful things. More than 27 years have passed since our first child was born, and the emotions, thoughts, and even a longing for that moment again are deep within me. I was there as this tiny new baby entered the world, contributing where I could and sharing every part of her new life. I still remember thinking, as we held her in those first hours, about what she would do, who she would become, and how she would maybe even change a part of our world. Ever hopeful and positive for the hopes and dreams of our new baby girl.

Being a father is difficult, sometimes even torturous, around young teenage girls. Our baby grew into a smart, attractive, headstrong, forthright, and popular 16-year-old girl. She was a whirlwind who embraced life and left no stone unturned. We saw these as great traits to guide her into adulthood, but she could be a challenge to parent as an adolescent and never accepted "no" well. This was the age when we noticed changes in her eating and exercise behaviour, and she became more controlling of every aspect of her life. She had lost a lot of weight. We sought professional help, which confirmed our worst fears that she had developed anorexia nervosa (AN). This began a long and drawn-out journey for all of us, battling an eating disorder (ED). We are incredibly grateful that her friends were vivacious and caring, and the ones we connected with would do anything for our daughter, and she would do anything for them. We are so grateful they stuck by her through it all and remain friends to this day.

Although I was so proud of her and everything she achieved, I was never far from trouble and never really able to do/say the right thing in her eyes. I found that she would always somehow keep me on edge, like I was walking on hot coals or very fragile eggshells. It was a strange connection, loving and being so proud of someone, but also never quite sure when she was going to stick her foot out and trip me up, leaving me at a loss, wondering what I'd done wrong.

When I was younger, finding my career path was not easy, but I have a passion for photography, pictures, cameras, lighting, and telling great stories. Being a news cameraman fulfilled those roles to a certain extent, although in another life I would have loved to be a filmmaker. My career was one of shiftwork, very long hours, starting early and finishing late, and many weekends not in a typical office as such. My office was a Toyota five-door, a large vehicle, and I cannot even imagine how many hours I spent in that car, driving more than 1,000,000 km over many years.

With my work, we were on the road, travelling to major unfolding events all over Victoria and sometimes interstate, covering them in time for the 6 p.m. news, then usually driving back in any weather conditions thrown our way. These trips were generally very stressful, but it was always satisfying when you met a major deadline and your story aired on the nightly news. Being in a car with another colleague for long hours was sometimes challenging, depending on who it was. Some journalists were very relaxed, and conversation flowed easily; others really weren't interested, preferring the company of their phones – those long drives were tough.

One afternoon, driving down the Monash freeway, my mobile rang with a distressing call from my wife, as events at home had escalated dramatically. She was in tears in our front bedroom, trying to distance herself, almost as an escape, from our daughter's eating disorder behaviour. From memory, we used to call this the witching hour, as it was predictable that when she arrived home from school and had not eaten, things would turn for the worse as the devil within her controlled her behaviour and thoughts, with no consideration for those around her. Throughout this time, we always thought this wasn't our daughter but the possessive and evil ED inside controlling her. The phone call lasted a few minutes, and she pleaded with me to get home as soon as possible.

The call was on speakerphone, as I drove through peak-hour traffic, and I remember my journalist quietly and calmly telling me to go home as soon as we got back to the office. By the time I got home, usually things had calmed down and resolved themselves to a reasonable level. Still, the stress, trauma, and anguish had already been created, not just for my wife but also our other child, who would hide in her bedroom, hoping it would all go away.

Being at work on those long days, weekends, public holidays, birthdays, and even Christmas Day was indeed difficult. There were certainly days at work when I felt very far away – worried, stressed, and even lonely. I worried that I wasn't contributing to what our family was going through and wasn't much help to anyone.

Time was valuable, so I enjoyed and prioritised my time with my daughter on my days off. Driving her to her social passions, including musical theatre, dance, and singing lessons, which took us to varied locations around Melbourne. This gave her much joy, freedom, and an escape to a different world, providing a short reprieve from her eating disorder. I believed these passions were contributing to her well-being and hoped they would help her escape from the shackles of her eating disorder. I was only too happy to be her chauffeur and give my wife a well-earned break. This was a way I felt I could really contribute, and often our father-daughter communication on these trips was easier. The driving hope for both of us was to help build a connection – a cornerstone of our future relationship.

In the car, it's an interesting dynamic. You don't sit facing each other, so eye contact remains brief; hence, our communication was better. We would generally talk carefully about activities at school, the subjects she was doing, her friends, and, most importantly, we would always enjoy music. The CD in the car was always loaded with a classic dad album or something she loved or had recommended to us. This was usually musical theatre. These times were very valuable in helping to build the fragile relationship, trying to nurture and keep alive what was an important connection between us.

As parents, we were incredibly proud of her achievements in schoolwork, but even more so to see her singing and "owning the stage" in her passion and skill for musical theatre. It was so important for us to embrace and enjoy these moments of escape from the other trauma that continuously surrounded us.

Amazingly, and to our surprise, our daughter was able to complete Year 12 with flying colours, even under the shadow and grip of the storm we were going through. Our conflict with what was happening was exacerbated and heightened by her ongoing deterioration in health. She was an inpatient in the hospital's eating disorder unit when she received her Year 12 results – an ATAR of 97.3, which could open the door to any career path she would like to pursue. She chose to study at ANU in Canberra. We rejoiced with her, but with a sense of dread. The anchor and structure of the school and our supportive paediatric ED team would all crumble when she left school and moved into a more adult style of care. This meant she had to agree to treatment, something she was reluctant to do.

The drive to Canberra from Melbourne is long, especially on a day with temperatures over 40 degrees in mid-February. We had tried to scaffold her life at ANU to keep her safe and prevent her from slipping through the gaps. We set up some "non-negotiables", including regular GP, psychologist, and dietitian appointments, as well as on-site accommodation with meals provided. Our anxiety was heightened when hearing about parents who had recently lost their child with an eating disorder at a university college in Sydney.

Our daughter revelled in university social and academic life but found it hard to keep the non-negotiables consistent for her monitoring and health. We did the best we could from such a distance, but my wife often received anxious calls and tears, and we suspected she was struggling more than she let on. Her health care team and university college refused to communicate with us about her health as they considered her an adult and their information confidential.

In April, I flew to Canberra for a theatre production of *Into the Woods* that she was proudly in, and, as always, I was excited to see her on stage. My excitement about our meeting after so many months had my mind totally blown when I saw a "stick figure" walking towards me. Apparently, this was supposed to be my daughter!!! I thought she had cancer. I shuddered at how sick she looked and how badly things had gone for her in Canberra, and I felt devastated. I tried to enjoy the musical production, but I honestly just wanted to look away. The eating disorder was in full flight. I was helpless to do anything and, as always, feared I might say something that could make things worse. My heart just ached at this relentless manifestation that had taken over our lives, and all I wanted to do was fix it. Protect her. Wasn't that my role as a father and a parent?

Doubting the decisions we had made and the weightlessness of her were frightening. Communication, honesty, and understanding were at an all-time low, but through all this, there was one message we needed her to hear very loudly and constantly. "We love you, we are trying to understand you, and we will never leave you. We will always be there beside you, fighting for you." This constant, unrelenting message is one I believe she did hear, though the possessive eating disorder would remain for several more years. We were in the muddy, disease-ridden trenches, and this was war!

Her days in Canberra had to end as she was simply too unwell, too far away from us and treatment. She came home and continued her studies. The following year was our lowest and hardest, but she had to keep going and always had hope that things would eventually, very slowly, turn around.

Unfortunately, my wife endured the most during these years. My support was haphazard, and home life was generally unpleasant, to say the least. Her medical knowledge and background as an allied health professional did her no favours, as she probably knew too much. Still, she always helped when talking to naive health professionals if they decided to listen. Most of the time, they thought they knew better than to listen to our concerns or to what our day-to-day lives were like. We were the classic case of falling through the gaps. Our mission on this journey was to ensure the system changed and that no one else should endure what we had been through.

Little ears can listen very well; walks with our dog became a significant activity as we would talk through the "battle" plan for each week, discussing self-care, new strategies, our other daughter's health, and, of course, upcoming medical appointments. Even with my irregular hours and shiftwork, we seemed to have enough time to discuss our strategy and direction in our movable "war room". Our younger daughter endured much, with relentless screaming, tension, yelling, and even some physical harm. Our daughters had never been close, but their relationship was entirely destroyed by anorexia at this time. She would hide in her room, which was her safe place, but sometimes just disappeared, usually walking around the block to have some quiet time to herself or finding a quiet place to talk to the dog, as he was an excellent listener. In hindsight, her care should have been a much higher priority.

The overall damage that eating disorders inflict on families is immense, and the importance of healing and rebuilding bridges cannot be underestimated. This process continues to this day, but certainly the scars run deep. Recovery wasn't just one thing. It's like a jigsaw puzzle where, annoyingly, some of the pieces are missing. My lack of insight and reluctance to learn certainly impeded my parenting for a while. Understanding and talking to fellow families going through a similar situation helped enormously. I suddenly realised we were not alone, and that we could help each other by asking insightful questions and sometimes hearing difficult responses. Frequently, events escalated beyond our control, and I didn't know how to de-escalate or move away from situations where emotions were rising. Some of these learnings seem logical and straightforward, but in the heat of battle, you just don't think straight. We completed a Skills-Based Carers course based on Janet Treasure's work, which proved invaluable. This helped us manage, validate, and understand the complexity of the eating disorder.

The other significant turning point in our family was, I believe, finding a peer mentor for our daughter. She was able to discredit everyone because, in her mind, they did not understand; they had not been there; they didn't see what she saw. This is legitimate, but her recovered peer mentor levelled the playing field immediately, and having a slightly older, mature, and pregnant woman as a healthy role model was a positive. This helped speed up her insight for recovery.

In 2020, during the COVID-19 lockdowns in Melbourne, our daily lives came to a halt. Our daughter, being the ultimate FOMO and party girl, was forced to slow down and spend more time alone, rather than running from one event to another. We lived within walking distance of her and would regularly spend one-on-one time with her, walking through our local parklands with the ever-present family dog. It was during this time that we could talk more frankly, and I found that our relationship started to improve. We had learnt not to focus on food and weight, and we used this time to discuss her other passions and dreams of travel and career, building a bigger picture of a healthier life. This allowed her to see beyond anorexia and her current situation and imagine a different future.

The one message we received from our daughter throughout this time was that she didn't feel she had a voice. Was this her speaking, or was it the eating disorder? I was never quite sure.

So many experiences were lost throughout this time; it should have been a very happy and joyous part of growing up, but instead, it was ripped away from us all. Everyone in the family had been affected. Every event, no matter how big or small, family, social, or holiday, would be tarnished by the presence of anorexia. Nothing was easy.

I discovered that a community meeting close by was reaching out to those with lived experience to share in the blueprint to take steps toward fixing – or at least improving – mental health outcomes in Victoria. Sharing my story obviously struck a chord with the organisers, who asked for more details about our harrowing experience in the health system. This whole process enabled my wife and me to share our story with the Victorian Royal Commission into Mental Health. Importantly, we were able to sit down with our daughter and ask her what she would say to the Commissioners if she had the chance. This gave her a powerful voice – one that would be listened to. At last, someone would listen to a family's experience of a day in the trenches. After an emotional presentation, the two of us were personally thanked by the Commissioners at the end of the day.

The three of us met up later for a drink, debriefing and celebrating what was a significant moment for us individually and as a family. We felt we were making a difference in some small way to the future of eating disorders. We hoped that our unfair plight would help many hundreds, if not thousands, who trod these paths of despair into the future.

By the grace of God, our daughter survived, and we are all here to occasionally remember, but more importantly, to write new experiences that will hopefully leave those dark days behind. New bridges have been built, and the battlements have been set on fire, left behind on a distant horizon. I now appreciate and carefully nurture stronger family relationships that will continue to blossom, and at last, I can enjoy some real family time. Our daughter is currently living her best life overseas. It is undoubtedly a great moment when she calls to say she misses us and looks forward to embracing us once again.

CHAPTER 8

Love Bears All Things

By Kelley Robertson

Love bears all things, believes all things, hopes all things, and endures all things. (Corinthians 13:7)

I have always believed in the resilient and protective nature of love. Love is willing to help carry burdens, shield from harm, and remain a steadfast constant through the most difficult times. This verse has been a guiding principle in my life, so much so that I have a tiny tattoo of it across my heart – Corinthians 13:7.

Throughout my 54 years, I have faced many challenges. I worked as a teacher in inclusive education and supported family members through complex mental health issues, addiction, and rehabilitation. I cared for my father, who had terminal melanoma, providing palliative care for him in my home. I even administered his last dose of morphine. During this time, I was also in the midst of a three-year IVF journey, which ultimately led to the birth of my beautiful daughter, Olivia, on 5 September 2003.

I can honestly say that none of these experiences compares to the immense courage it takes to support someone you love who is battling an eating disorder.

When Olivia was 15, she became unwell with anorexia. This was seven years ago, and the treatment and support options available then were vastly different from those available now. What started as a seemingly mild issue quickly escalated into a severe and enduring illness, resulting in six years of continuous medical and mental health ward admissions. It still surprises me how quietly the illness began, masked by the guise of something positive – getting her life back on track after my 17-year marriage collapsed, which had devastated every aspect of our family. The perfect storm of relocation, divorce, family court, and Olivia being used as a pawn was overwhelming.

As we tried to piece our lives back together, I worked 40 hours a week while my daughter returned to her studies and embraced a health kick, focusing on clean eating and a fitness regimen. Social media added an additional layer of reinforcement with the abundant praise for her achievements. Being a perfectionist, she finished Year 10 with an A+ report card, received a prize for English, and simultaneously developed the most severe eating disorder.

And I had missed the signs. Looking back, I have many "if only" moments.

Olivia's weight loss was hidden under baggy clothing, and it wasn't until we visited the emergency room after she collapsed and was admitted for refeeding syndrome that I truly understood the extent of her struggle. When I helped her in the shower that night, I was shocked by what I saw; she had all but vanished. I couldn't believe what "she" had done to herself. I remember feeling my knees buckle and wanting to scream, but I knew I couldn't for Olivia's sake. She was terrified and ashamed, and her secret was now laid bare. I swallowed my horror deeply and remained outwardly calm, even as my mind screamed in anguish.

This wouldn't be the only time I faced such a moment over the next six years, but love bears all things.

Initially, I had a simplistic view: we just needed to go back to how things were, and that meant eating. I had no real understanding of how difficult that would be. I remember the first time the NG tube was to be inserted. The fear in her eyes was palpable as she pleaded, "I can eat; please just let me." But she wasn't allowed to eat. Her body had degenerated to the point where her organs were shutting down. Nutrients needed to be administered slowly and continuously, or her body would go into shock, and she could die – an outcome I hadn't known was even a possibility.

I told her, "The only choice you have right now is how you're going to do this. You can fight the tube, or you can face this with the same grace and dignity you have shown your entire life." Those words were profound.

Thus, we began our journey, though I had no idea what lay ahead and was far from fully prepared.

One of the most misunderstood aspects of an eating disorder is that its primary effect is outward weight loss; however, the unseen issue is the loss of cognitive function. The body draws what it needs from every organ, including the brain. Therefore, you are asking someone with limited cognitive capacity to do the unthinkable. The primitive part of the brain gets stuck in fight-or-flight mode, filled with extreme anxiety, while logic and reasoning seem to vanish.

At that time, I was unaware of this and approached the situation aggressively. As the noise escalated, I raised my voice, but she couldn't hear me.

"Anna" (as we named the eating disorder) became a formidable barrier between Olivia and me. Her illness convinced her that I was the enemy. It truly despised me, and I felt as if I needed more than just holy water to combat it. I needed a chair and a whip to defend myself against it, and I fought back fiercely. At other times, I would see Olivia disengage, listening to "Anna".

During those moments, I would say, "If you're talking to it, tell it that your mother is coming for it, and it should be scared." Olivia would often reply, "You don't understand, Mum," and then shut down, retreating into her own world.

Despite the daunting road ahead, I held onto the belief that love could bear it all. We fought together tirelessly, and I knew deep down that, with time, understanding, and unwavering support, we could overcome it. The journey may have been long and filled with obstacles, but through love, we found hope and resilience.

As I had to work full-time, I would leave work and spend my nights and every weekend with my daughter at the hospital. As a single mother, I was all she had. My sole purpose was to try to reclaim my girl and keep her connected to herself and to my love. Any spare time I had was spent researching.

I clearly remember the morning I found a TED Talk by Dr Laura Hill called "Eating Disorders from the Inside Out". For the first time, I understood the eating disorder from Olivia's perspective – the anxiety, the disturbance, and "the noise". I also realised my own noise was contributing to her struggle. I rushed to the hospital and played the TED Talk for Olivia. The relief on her face was priceless and encouraging. She now knew that I understood the enemy and that I was in her corner.

By that time, Olivia had been in the hospital for over a year, and the time spent there had only reinforced one thing she could control: her eating disorder. Mental health wards can be soul-crushing. It's not a happy place, sitting in your own pain while hearing and seeing everyone else's day and night. Finding love in that space was extremely hard.

I filled her room with a picture board showcasing all the things she was, the things she loved, and the people who loved her – reasons to keep fighting, reasons to not vanish. I put short, powerful mantras on the wall that we repeated over and over. I did everything I could to try to keep her connected to herself and to the strength of my love.

"Anna", the eating disorder, always told Olivia she had to keep moving; it was relentless. Every visit, I would try to get Olivia to rest with me on her bed. She would resist at first, but when she finally did, she would wrap her arms and legs around me and fall instantly asleep. My tiny, fragile girl, with a tube in place and her heart monitor beeping, would be wrapped in my protective arms, her head resting on my heart for hours. I would not move until she woke.

I always brought a scarf with me when I went to see her, and she would always ask, "Can I keep it, Mum? It smells of you." I bought her stuffed toys, but not all of them were cuddly. Kenny the Koala was the best. He was ugly and fierce; his stitched face was one only a mother could love. I entrusted him to be there for Olivia when I wasn't. I told her to hug him tight when "Anna" came in. I even gave him a voice – deep and strong: "Fuck off, Anna, nobody likes you."

I did everything I could to make my girl laugh. I became a comedic genius, trying to find the humour in the pain we faced every day, so much so that humour became my default response instead of crying. It was exhausting to be fearless in the face of terror – through rounds with "Anna", endless family meetings with doctors, and advocating for a better fit of care and recovery model because the punitive treatment we had clearly wasn't working.

With the punitive model of treatment, the longest time without leave was four months. Cut off from life, family, and friends, it only served to escalate her eating disorder cognitions further. It was no longer just about restriction and excessive exercising. I watched my girl disappear before my eyes, totally consumed by her illness. It was a constant battle in her head, and I was up against the fiercest opponent I had ever met, with the stakes at their highest.

She was the worst case the hospital had. Constant one-on-one nursing was required, and when she was discharged home, I likened myself to a commando on a mission – living on caffeine and adrenaline, with little or no sleep and always keeping one eye open. All the while, I hoped I could get one clear shot at the enemy. We tried so hard in the small window we had before "Anna" grabbed her hand again and led her back to hell.

My father, when he was alive, always said to me when choosing friends, "Imagine you are going to war; who would you take with you?" Luckily, I had made some excellent choices of people to call my best friends (most of them lifelong), and they all came in to pick up the baton of love and hope, each with their own unique strengths and enormous love for me and my child. We were indeed in the trenches, going over the top together.

It was often one step forward and five steps back. There were many times we nearly lost her. I arrived at the children's hospital after morning handover to see nurses crying. Administration had told them to prepare for Olivia's death. At that moment, everything became very real for me. I was so angry. How dare they give up hope when that was all we had? I would not accept it. I refused to believe it. We were not going to lie down and die; we still had fight left in us, and it was imperative that everyone, especially those at the hospital, were on the same page. Yet, those words haunted me in the early hours of the morning. What if they were right?

It was then that I realised that, as much as I wanted to fix this, it was going to have to come from Olivia, and I could not do it for her. Olivia has always been a fighter, and I just had to remind her of her power.

So, I wrote a poem to her:

Fading before my eyes
in the wrath of its grip
oblivious to what I see.

Struggling, fighting, believing the lies
the constant voice in your head
telling you that you are not enough.

Perfection in my memories
watching it destroy your potential
your beauty, all that you are and are yet to become.

I would reach inside you
and pull it from you if I could
bear your pain across my back and
destroy this insidious disease.

My love is powerful
but not enough
it is all I have, and it is yours.

Treading water
bobbing up and down
it is time to swim
the hardest race of your life.

I cannot lead you there
but I will swim in your glorious wake
every stroke of the way.

Willing you to fight
willing you to believe in you
with a life ahead of you.

A life that you can steer
a life that you deserve
claim it, my daughter
you are enough.

As a transfer to the adult system loomed, we found ourselves trapped in a system that felt voiceless, deemed non-compliant and treatment-resistant with a treatment order. I desperately sought access to the private system, but the severity and complexity of my child's illness meant that no one would accept us. We were stuck, facing a predicted outcome that left me terrified. All we had was love and hope.

At 18 years old, cognitively delayed and barely medically stable, my child was admitted to the adult system, not fit for purpose. There was no specialised eating disorder ward, and the doctors and nurses had limited training in managing cases as complex as Olivia's. My access was restricted to just one hour a day. My plan to maintain a connection with my child faced an enormous roadblock. On days when I couldn't visit, I would jump the fence to see her through the window of her room, placing my hand on the reinforced glass while she did the same. We shared an unspoken conversation, and I hoped she knew: "I am here. You can do this. I am here."

Olivia's admission was catastrophic and detrimental. The treatment we both received on that ward bordered on human rights violations. Although there was one-on-one nursing, the shifts were only an hour long due to burnout. Olivia was the most unwell I had ever seen her; she had dissociated, and throughout this ordeal, my voice was discounted, pathologised, and dismissed. She spent 18 months in what could only be described as a holding pen, surrounded by a culture of cruelty. She was a young girl with an eating disorder, not a prisoner. She had done nothing wrong and nothing to deserve what happened to her in that place.

The portrayal of mental health wards often depicted in movies is true; I had not known such places existed. Leaving my severely ill child in an unsafe environment devoid of love and human compassion nearly destroyed me. But love endures all things.

When discharge came, her psychiatrist refused my plea for a gradual return to the community. I was told Olivia would have to find her own way, but she didn't have the resources to do so. As a vulnerable person who had been warehoused for five years without therapeutic support, compounded by trauma and a dysregulated nervous system, she ran as far away from safety, me, as she could. She left home, associated with the wrong crowd, and engaged in polydrug use to numb her pain and quiet the eating disorder voice.

Now an adult with the treatment order removed, I had no say. The day she asked me to drop her at the train station, I struggled to find words. I had to let her go and watch everything unravel. I could only plant the seed that she would eventually find her way back home. "Don't get so far in that you can't get yourself out."

Every aspect of our lives crumbled. My girl was lost to me, and I could no longer shield her from harm. She was out in the darkness, searching for herself. For many months, I waited in terror, completely out of control. Then one early morning, I received a call: "Mum, I think I'm going to die. Help me."

So, I packed two bags, and we went interstate. We needed to cut ties with people and things that did not serve her, as there was no help for us at home. It was radical practice; we had tried going interstate briefly before, but now had one final shot to turn this situation around. After enduring severe carer burnout, I had to dig deep to fight not just against "Anna" but also against the trauma it had brought with it.

I found a GP to monitor her observations, and for the next ten months, it was a 24/7 effort. There was no support for eating disorders interstate, which made it incredibly challenging. Our family psychiatrist provided support via telehealth appointments as we navigated psychosis and catatonia while working to stabilise her weight.

I am immensely proud of my fierce daughter. I didn't heal her; she did that herself. My love was the anchor. With the right time, space, and tools, she began to move forward. The day her brain was nourished and the light returned to her eyes after being in the dark for so long was one of the most beautiful moments of my life, rivalling her birth.

A mother's fierce love and understanding of her child, grounded in lived experience and years of intensive research, armed me with a wealth of knowledge through various resources, podcasts, programs, and carer forums. I drew on what was relevant to support her recovery, using techniques that would resonate with her. We worked our way out of the vortex, ensuring we had enough distance to avoid being sucked back in, and began the journey of recovery.

Two years have passed, and it isn't all cups of tea and

laughter. Recovery is not as simple as weight restoration and returning to how things were. I have witnessed an extraordinary demonstration of human courage, resilience, and strength as I watched my daughter pick up her sword and fight her way back to herself. She has never been a daddy's princess; she has always been her mother's fierce warrior.

Life must be rebuilt, and that takes time, understanding, compassion for oneself, and unconditional love for one another. We are no longer lost; we are simply in a transitional phase. We are not who we once were, nor are we yet who we will become. It's like a gentle incoming tide – slow and steady, yet full of hope, belief, and enduring love.

CHAPTER 9

On the Inside

By Fiona Carusi

Her eyes were hollow, dark, soulless. She hadn't showered for days, her hair tangled, her skin colourless. She didn't blink. Didn't move. She just stared blankly. I looked deep – but saw nothing. My heart was broken, my body exhausted, and my mind lost.

My beautiful, precious girl, where are you?

She glared into her lap as her tears fell silently. Her hands sat under the table; her dinner lay perfectly on the plate. Untouched.

The sun had gone down by now, and we sat across the table in the shadows. Light flickered from the other room while the TV murmured in the background. The news reported yet another lockdown. It seemed the world was united in distress, but not us; we were disconnected, battling our own kind of anguish, alone, and in silence.

Oh Lord, how the hell did we get here?

My phone vibrated quietly nearby. I didn't care and let it ring out. The outside world felt blurred, distant … like it didn't exist. Family and friends kept reaching out, but every conversation only stirred up more anxiety. I tried to explain what we were going through, but my words were too weak and too muddled to capture the chaos inside. It left me with nothing but emptiness and frustration. Avoiding it was just easier.

That night, she fell asleep in my arms. Clenching tightly like it was the only safe place on earth. My body was twisted and restless, but I lay still. The truth was that holding on to her gave me comfort, too.

I stroked her gritty hair, and for a fleeting moment, I was transported back six years to a better, brighter world. She was eight, full of excitement over the plaits she wanted for her disco-themed birthday party. She looked delightful that day, twirling in her tulle rainbow dress, a true picture of happiness and health. She was always smiling, always carefree, and always looking for fun. That was another time entirely, a different girl. That girl was long gone ... lost and wasted away.

I woke up to the humming of my phone.

"Hubby," it read. Glowing was his smiling image of an era that felt lost in time. I slowly peeled her arm from my waist and crept out of the room.

"Another rough one?" he asked.

"Hmm ..." was all I could manage to mutter.

Hubby worked in the construction industry and was exempt from the lockdowns. Each day, when he left for work, he escaped the chaos that raged within our home. For most of the day, he escaped to a world that still made some sense. Meanwhile, we were trapped. Me, the children, the fear, the suffocation, and the dread. He didn't experience it the way I did. He couldn't. I felt unbearably alone.

In moments like this, it usually felt like he was the only thing holding me together. Yet this time, even his strength couldn't reach the worry tearing through me. I wanted to scream, to pour everything out, but I had neither the energy nor the will. I could only mutter that I would take her back to the hospital.

"But they said she's okay," he offered gently.

"SHE'S NOT OKAY!" I barked, instantly regretting the outburst. He didn't push back.

"Okay, okay ... let me know how you go," he conceded.

Reaching the hospital, I lifted her weak, limp body and

settled her gently into a wheelchair. Her clothes hung loosely on her frail frame, and she could barely hold herself up. She slumped over as I pushed her toward the emergency room.

"You have one very sick little girl here," the triage nurse whispered as she took our details and listed the symptoms. Her eyes were knowing. It settled me somehow, a glimmer of understanding amid all the judgement.

After patiently waiting for what felt like a lifetime, we were taken into a consulting room. I was full of optimism.

Okay, this is it. Make them understand … Lord, help me make them understand.

I told our story. I was clear, direct, and tried hard not to sound hysterical. The doctor seemed to understand. There was plenty of nodding and a few thoughtful questions. Everything was carefully noted and placed in a manila folder. For the first time, I felt reassured.

As night fell, the weight of the day settled over me. The beeping of her heart monitor and her gentle breathing were strangely soothing. I folded my arms over her bed, rested my head, and drifted into a light sleep.

Out of nowhere, the doctor's roaring voice tore through the calm. Urgent and terrifying, yanking me straight into a panic.

"Okay!" he boomed. "You can go home now."

Home? No, no, no, no. She can't go home!!

A rush of adrenaline came over me, and panic clawed at my throat. I wanted to shake him up and tear down the hospital walls! Yet nothing came out. There was nothing but disbelief and a soul-shattering helplessness.

SAY SOMETHING … SPEAK!!!!

"Why are we going home?" I asked, barely above a whisper. He didn't flinch. Didn't hesitate.

"Her vitals are normal. No need to take up a bed."

Every bone in my body wanted to scream out.

You've GOT to be kidding me! The girl can hardly stand!

"I don't understand," I said, my voice raw and shaky.

"Her numbers are within the normal range," he repeated, flat and mechanical. "We can only admit her if they fall below."

With that, he closed the file shut with a sound that resonated like a final verdict. He turned and walked out.

At that moment, I broke. Then and there, I felt like a part of me fell on the hospital floor.

* * *

Countless medical appointments followed; dietitians, GPs, psychologists, paediatricians – and a few more desperate trips to the emergency room. Each visit brought hope, and each ended in disappointment. For a long time, we searched tirelessly for a team of professionals who could truly help us, but every door seemed to close. Each rejection cut deeper, leaving me more exhausted, more anxious, more alone. It was a weight that threatened to crush me, a puzzle that seemed impossible to solve.

Months passed, and seasons turned. We went out less, smiled less, and celebrated less. The joy that once filled our home was dimmed, replaced by a quiet heaviness that lingered in every corner of our lives. This disease imprisoned us, trapped in our own home and in our own heads, waiting for answers that never came.

Well-meaning voices kept giving us advice. Endless advice. They all thought themselves experts on something, it seemed, they knew absolutely nothing about. I tried to listen, hoping for something, some thread of understanding. But their counsel only left me angrier and more conflicted. I felt constantly misunderstood, shamed, and … to be honest … judged. They couldn't see how fragile everything was, how their attempts to help only deepened the wound. Defending myself felt impossible, like screaming in a language no one could understand.

One friend felt the need to tell me she thought I wasn't strict enough and that I was spoiling my children. It wouldn't have happened in her house, she said. She had control of her kids. The words landed like a fist to the stomach, stealing the breath from my lungs.

The nerve! What did she know? How dare she insult my parenting!

I knew she wouldn't understand. This wasn't about discipline; it was something else entirely. Something sinister. It was a poison buried so deep and so cleverly under the radar that it embedded itself into us without warning. Even she would have been powerless against it.

Another time, someone else claimed that restrictive eating came from a controlling mother.

I wanted to scream, to lash out, but my body just froze. My feet cemented to the floor. Nothing came out. I just stood there, burning, and wished she would disappear.

I started questioning myself – was she right? I did insist my kids keep their room clean, and I nagged about things that now seemed so painfully insignificant.

Maybe she was right. Perhaps I was too controlling. Or maybe I was too soft? Which one was it???!!! The conversations looped endlessly in my head.

Oh God, what did I do? Too much control … no, not enough.

Me. Not me. Me! Stop. Stop. Stop. MAKE IT STOP. MAKE THEM ALL STOP!

* * *

Many more months passed – months of watching her fade, of nights spent hovering outside her door, listening for the slightest sign that she was okay, terrified she might hurt herself. Those months stretched into years. We lived suspended in fear and exhaustion, trapped in an endless cycle of crisis and despair.

Most nights, I found myself watching, waiting, listening, holding my breath. Fear had become routine. I recall one night, the shower stopped. She emerged from the steam, pale and trembling, weaker than I'd ever seen her. My heart sank. I braced myself, and before either of us spoke, we were racing back to the hospital.

Yet again, the doctor saw me as just another overdramatic mother. I felt the crushing weight of misjudgement, another person waving away my fears.

"She's only feeling unwell because she had a hot shower," was the protest this time.

At that instant, it became clear. No one was going to save her, so I had to step out of my comfort zone and take charge.

* * *

Barrier after barrier – they were unyielding and cruel. But I didn't give up. Somehow, I kept fighting. Each setback became a quiet teacher, revealing something new and strengthening a resilience I never knew I had. Every long drive home, heavy with uncertainty, became a testament to endurance.

Over time, I realised she was watching me, observing how I reacted, asking questions, quietly learning. Slowly, she began to follow my lead. I learned to stand taller in the face of frustration, and she watched. I started to trust my instincts, and she followed. I held space for hope, even when it felt so very fragile, and she did, too.

Somewhere along the way, we became a team – learning, growing, fighting together. Every closed door became a reason to look deeper, push harder, and speak louder. Together, we grew stronger, and in the end, she slowly started to heal.

To say this was the toughest fight our family has ever faced would be a staggering understatement. Nothing could have prepared us for what we endured. Even now, we remain alert, watching in case the dreaded beast dares to rear its ugly head again. But if it does, this time, it won't stand a chance. This time, we are stronger and ready.

If this journey has taught me anything, it is never to hold back. Your voice is your weapon. Stay strong and trust your instincts. When your intuition screams, you listen. You advocate. You hold tight, and you fight like your life depends on it. Even when your heart is breaking, even when your voice shakes, even when the world seems blind – you fight. You persist. You rise. Because sometimes, holding on is the only way … and through that fight, you find yourself again – braver, louder, and unbreakable.

CHAPTER 10

Your Superpowers

By Alanna McInerney

On the cusp of her 30th birthday, our daughter is living in Amsterdam with her loving, supportive partner as she continues to recover. Life is not perfect, but is it for anyone really? She lost her adolescence and young adulthood to anorexia nervosa (AN) and, since starting recovery three years ago, has been catching up on the life skills most young women have mastered by this age. No one really talks about how life stands still when you have severe and enduring anorexia nervosa (SEAN) for 14 years. Still, it does, both for the loved one and for those doing the loving.

Our daughter is learning how to live in the world as an adult. She is learning to organise her days, to develop and maintain friendships, to apply for a job, to trust herself, and to find healthy and well-adapted ways to deal with stress instead of retreating into the eating disorder (ED) as a familiar and "safe" place to hide. She knows now that it's not, and by finding better ways to deal with life's challenges, it's losing its power. She feels much safer now, but recovery is not linear. She knows the eating disorder lingers in the dark corners of her psyche, always on the alert for opportunities. She knows that continued vigilance is needed to make the right choices to maintain and develop her wellness. It's much easier now to make healthy choices because life offers her so much more. She can participate in and contribute to her own life and those of the people who surround and love her. The rewards of making healthy choices are so much greater. I have the deepest respect for her as she slowly navigates her way back into the life she wants.

This isn't a story about our daughter, but rather a story about the superpowers we possess as carers. I can almost hear you thinking, "What superpowers? On the contrary, I feel utterly powerless against this raging storm!" I understand. I've been where you are. It is only now, on the other side, that I can identify the power we held, knowing it sustained us through the hardest and darkest times in our lives, preparing us to be ready and able when the time came to recover. Your superpowers may be different to ours, but I believe they are there, and I hope that sharing ours with you may help you find your own. Our four superpowers, in no particular order, were and continue to be: the relentless refusal to give up; our unconditional love; our choice to be humble and open ourselves to continually learn about the eating disorder and its impact on our loved one and our family; and, finally, our choice to truly listen to and hear our daughter. In my experience, when combined with a team of dedicated, highly skilled eating disorder specialists, these are the keys to recovery. Whatever your superpowers may be, identify them and use them relentlessly.

When our outrageously loud, energetic, and fun-loving daughter disappeared and was replaced by a secretive, exhausted shadow of herself, it wasn't easy to remain positive, to love unconditionally, to listen, or to want to learn about the eating disorder, which we hated passionately. We didn't understand what was happening. We just wanted our girl back. The more we fought it, the deeper she retreated.

We sought help but couldn't find any service that met our needs in the early years. Children's hospital outpatient services, private psychologists, family therapists – she had them wrapped around her little finger. Like many people with eating disorders, our daughter is clever. She became an expert at saying the "right" things to her therapists to make them think she was recovering, only to keep losing weight and eventually again be admitted to hospital. After about four years, we were lucky to find a psychiatrist who had her number from the outset. Later, she talked of the immense relief she felt when she first met him and realised he couldn't be manipulated by the eating disorder. For the first time, she thought there may be some hope. Nevertheless, it would be another ten years until she could find the strength to try to recover.

This brings us to our first superpower: never give up on hope. The eating disorder is frightened of our hope and works incessantly to destroy it, thriving on hopelessness. I tried to look beyond it to the girl I knew was still there. By repeatedly doing this, I remembered who she really was and how much I knew she wanted to get better, even when she said she didn't, even when she abused us for trying to help her. It's probably the hardest thing we've ever done – trying to remain hopeful, always believing our daughter could recover, and telling her over and over again.

One day, when she was well into recovery and had been overseas for a few months, I saw her psychiatrist by chance. It was my first opportunity since recovery had begun to thank him for what he had done for her over the past ten years. He smiled and replied gently, "I just never gave up. I always believed she could recover." In doing this, we hold the space, the love and the hope for them that they cannot hold for themselves. They are drowning in self-loathing, despair, and hopelessness. Holding this space for our daughter gave us a sense of power that kept us going through the darkest days.

Over time, I came to understand that I held another super-power: unconditional love. Unconditional love doesn't mean letting your loved one behave however they like, or letting them treat you and others badly, even as they flounder in the morass of an eating disorder. For us, it meant setting boundaries that reflect the respect you have for yourself, for others, and for them. It meant listening to her, understanding, not judging. It meant acknowledging her pain and allowing her to express it without confusing it with our guilt. It meant holding her when she'd let us, despite the terror her tiny frame ignited in us. It meant being kind and compassionate when all we wanted to do was scream. Perhaps most of all, it meant apologising and asking for forgiveness whenever we just plain could not, and did not, do these things.

Carers know that the eating disorder changes our loved ones, often into someone who's not easy to like, a secretive combatant intent on their own and, it feels, our destruction. Trust, the stalwart of a strong relationship, disappears. In its place comes screaming, crying and yelling, unbearable silences, cruel words, lies, threats, and sometimes even physical violence. All of this makes your loved one feel like an enemy and almost impossible to like. This is precisely what the eating disorder wants, so you will give up, go away, and let it do its worst. Please don't do that. Instead, find and hang on for dear life to the person you know is still there and the deep, unbreakable love you feel for them despite all these challenges.

Unconditional love gives you more power than you know. Over time, it rebuilt the trust that had been lost between us in the early years when we struggled to understand and support her. It allowed our daughter to eventually feel safe enough to go against the eating disorder and ask for our help to recover. She often tells us she could never have done it alone. We became her truth during recovery when she could not trust herself, as the eating disorder fought back, trying to derail her progress. She repeatedly asked us, "Am I doing the right thing?" She trusted us when we said repeatedly, "Yes, it's absolutely the right thing to do. No question." She had lived with our unconditional love and was now using it as an anchor in her storm.

We've all heard it many times throughout our lives – knowledge is power. For us, it was our third superpower and is deeply entwined with the others. Without knowledge and understanding of the eating disorder and its impact on all of us, we may not have survived as a family. If we'd buried our heads in the sand, hoping it would all just go away, we would not be where we are today. It would have been almost impossible to remain hopeful and to love unconditionally. Opening ourselves to learning about the eating disorder demonstrated our hope and our love for our daughter in a very practical, humble way. As a few evidence-based studies and resources emerged and people started to talk more about eating disorders, we began to understand and have insight into what it was like for her. We learned, most importantly, that it is an illness and never a lifestyle choice.

In 2018, our daughter contributed to the ANGI study, the largest-ever genetic study of anorexia nervosa. ANGI identified DNA variations thought to contribute to the risk for anorexia nervosa and opened the door to understanding it as a psychiatric-metabolic illness. Although the findings have not yet changed clinical practice, for us, they provided a breakthrough in our understanding of this eating disorder – how we supported her, how we spoke to her, the words we used, the decisions we made about treatment options and other aspects of her care.

Despite the desperate need for more evidence-based research, it was a big relief to finally have some science to guide us.

Seeing us reach out for resources and advice, and implement useful strategies, also helped restore trust in our relationship, and eventually our daughter started to share her own story and lived experience with us. It is from her that I learned most about the eating disorder, and surprisingly, at the time, the most about myself. I learned that she was plagued with thoughts of self-disgust and hatred that were quieter when she gave in to them and overwhelming when she tried to go against them. I learned of her crippling shame, her guilt about putting all those she loved most through such torment. I learned how isolated, alone, and misunderstood she felt, and how utterly powerless she felt to change any of it. She helped me learn about myself – how I wanted to defend rather than listen and learn.

Deep down, I knew I had been hiding from some difficult truths. We both knew some of my decisions, although not the cause of her eating disorder, had been sitting silently between us like a veil. My knee-jerk reaction was to defend myself, which only antagonised my daughter and further eroded trust between us. Hearing and understanding her perspective helped me own those decisions, both a painful and freeing process for me. Talking about them with her lifted the veil and brought us so much closer.

Eating Disorders Families Australia (EDFA) and other organisations now have comprehensive resources for carers; however, when our daughter first developed anorexia nervosa, information was scattered, contradictory, and confusing. At one point, in desperation, we reached out to an "expert" in the USA who, upon learning our daughter's story, advised us to give her an ultimatum: either she ate or she had to leave home.

It was expected that the ultimatum would force recovery and circumvent her departure, but what if it didn't? She was just 16 and deep within the eating disorder. We could not reconcile this approach with our knowledge of anorexia nervosa, a psychiatric-metabolic illness. Neither could we be the architects of our daughter's homelessness in the event the eating disorder was too powerful, and she had no choice but to leave. So, we chose to ignore this "advice".

In our view, our daughter needed to be wrapped in our superpowers to survive and eventually begin to recover, and this has fortunately been borne out. Years later, I told her about this incident. Chillingly, she said she would have had no choice but to leave at that time – the voices were far too strong. I cannot dare to think where she may be now if we had given her that ultimatum. This experience, although disturbing, taught us how important it is to learn as much as you can and follow the instincts you develop from that knowledge.

Our fourth superpower was listening to understand rather than to solve, and it was very difficult for me. As her mother, my instinct was to protect her at all costs, fix her pain, make everything okay. After all, she is my baby! How wrong could I have been! My desperation to see her well translated into endless suggestions for recovery that only reinforced to my daughter how little I truly understood her. My proffered solutions infuriated and isolated her. For a long time, I didn't realise that what she needed from us was to be heard, her pain acknowledged and accepted. She didn't want advice; she didn't think she could be "fixed".

One day, she was sitting on my knee, and as usual, I was making suggestions and giving her advice I hoped might help. To my bewilderment, she told me to stop and suddenly buried her face in my shoulder, sobbing uncontrollably. I stopped talking, and finally I just listened. When I stopped trying to fix her, she started to share, very slowly and carefully, her own nightmare, and I began to understand what she was going through and how we could really help her.

One day, when trust had been restored, she came to me and, in a tiny voice, whispered, "Mum, I'm so hungry." She could never have admitted this to me before, and I was simultaneously shattered and relieved. She was giving me a glimpse into her world. She was starving, and she could not feed herself. I could not feed her. I desperately wanted to suggest she eat one of her "safe" foods, but I knew that wasn't what she needed from me, so I simply put my arms around her, cried with her, and listened while she told me how she felt. That was what she needed from me, to hold her, to listen, to see and love her as she really was.

We have another beautiful daughter, a loving, generous soul who was, and continues to be, a tremendous support to her sister. They have always been very close, maybe because of losing their father, my husband, when they were just three and six, maybe just because of the people they are, or possibly both. Sometimes I think the sibling carer role can be the most difficult, and our daughter would probably agree to some extent. Unlike parents who have responsibility for their children's safety, siblings may feel they have a choice to distance themselves. Walking away, however, was not an option for her despite feeling lonely, isolated, overwhelmed, terrified, angry, and guilty for much of the time during those years.

She talks of the immense contradictions that exist in your mind when you are cooking dinner for the third time that evening because the first two attempts did not meet the stringent requirements of the eating disorder, or when you are being insulted for ruining your sister's life when you have almost given up on your own to help save theirs. During these harrowing times, you ask yourself, "Why am I doing this? Is it worth it?" The answer is always, "Yes, it's worth it."

When we're in the trenches, it is often near impossible to see that life can be any different, but it can. She embraced her own superpowers to help both herself and her sister through those very dark years. It is not easy. Everyone is different, and everyone responds differently. There is no place for judgement of those doing their best in the world of eating disorders, regardless of their role. After putting parts of her life on hold to care for her sister, it's now wonderful to see her thriving, living with a lovely partner in London. People ask how we manage with both our daughters living overseas. My response is always the same – of course, we miss them; however, the joy of seeing them both living their best lives after so many hard years is so wonderful! One of the greatest ongoing pleasures and rewards of recovery for our daughter is seeing her family living full and joyous lives again.

ARFID Journey

By Shannon McGlinchey

Food …

For me, food is a gastronomical experience. I can predict the taste of every spoonful before it hits my mouth. For my son, it's the opposite. He finds it frightening, anxiety rising even at the thought. For him, food is not nourishment – it's fear.

This is our journey with ARFID (avoidant/restrictive food intake disorder), and if you're reading this as a fellow carer, know you're not alone. There is hope.

The Dream Beginning That Changed

December 1st, 2018 – the best day of our lives. Five pregnancy tests confirmed what I'd dreamed: I was going to be a mum. I cruised through pregnancy with ease, maintaining a healthy diet, exercising regularly, and working until the week before the birth. "I've got this," I would say to myself.

As a baby, my son was a dream: a great feeder, an amazing sleeper, and the happiest little soul. Parenting seemed easy. But around age two, everything changed. He began rejecting foods overnight, even his favourites. Berries, yoghurt, and salmon, which had once delighted him, suddenly made him gag.

I became the mum constantly asking others about their children's eating, taking him to doctors with my concerns. Each visit yielded the same dismissive response: "It's just a picky eating phase. He'll grow out of it." But mother's intuition was screaming, "This is different." My son wasn't just fussy – he was anxious, even fearful.

When I first heard about ARFID through a client whose child had been diagnosed, everything clicked. Her experiences mirrored ours exactly. By this point, we were down to the bare minimum of food, nothing of nutritional value, and would happily skip meals at age three. Armed with information, I returned to our doctor. "I think my son has ARFID." He had to look it up. Because my son was still technically "eating" something, we didn't get very far.

Lesson One: Trust your instincts. You know your child best. Keep detailed food diaries, document behaviours, and advocate fiercely even when professionals dismiss your concerns. You're not being dramatic. You're being a parent.

When Life Throws Curveballs

In 2022, we discovered we were adding to our family, another miracle. My boy was beside himself with joy, telling us how much he already loved his sister. I hoped this would encourage him to explore food again.

This pregnancy was rough: terrible morning sickness, no energy, gastro sweeping through the house. By now, he had lost almost all "safe" foods. Looking back, I tried to identify triggers: gastro outbreaks, a choking incident with a paper sachet. Could such small events have such a huge impact on a young child?

Then tragedy struck. On May 7, 2022, I woke hourly from dreams plagued by death. When my mum's best friend called instead of her, panic set in. My baby sister tragically lost her life at 41. "How will I explain this to my son? Will this set us back?"

The following day, we tested positive for COVID-19. I was mourning my sister, growing a baby, sick to the high heavens, and attempting to plan a funeral from my bed. My son saw me break down countless times. He would tell people, "Mum lost her best friend, and she cries a lot." My little empath comforted me while I worried about the stress fuelling his food issues.

When his baby sister arrived, tears of joy filled his eyes. He had gained a sister while I had lost mine. He'd sit with me during feeds, asking a million questions about food and what babies eat. Finally, we were talking freely about food. Yet he regressed, wanting only bottles of milk for breakfast, lunch, and dinner. Our first round of liquid-only meals.

Lesson Two: Stress is ARFID's best friend. Major life events can trigger regression. You can't shield them from everything. During crises, focus on maintaining safe foods rather than expanding.

The Educational Battlefield

Three-year-old kindergarten should have been easy. My son thrived in occasional care; he was known as the king of the kids where he was, where the fun was! But his first day of three-year-old kinder involved a major altercation that set the tone for the year. He'd come from gentle encouragement to rigid rules and standards. His light dimmed daily. But the worst part was their obsession with his eating.

"Oh, he's so frustrating to watch eat, the most painful child I've ever taught."

"We spent money on the healthy eating program, and all the children participated except yours."

I pulled him out and let him choose his new kindergarten. Best decision ever! Amazing, empathetic educators, solid friendships forming, and dare I say it, he started to explore food again. Maybe he didn't have a problem; he just needed his people and place.

Then tonsillitis struck, three times in six months. Each bout meant complete food refusal due to throat pain; each recovery, fewer safe foods returned. We were back in our private hell, but now with the added pressure of approaching school age.

Lesson Three: Environment is everything. One unsupportive educator can undo months of progress. Ask kindergartens and schools about their approach to eating difficulties. Ask specific questions: How do you handle children who don't eat? What happens during food-based activities? Seek educators who see your child, not just their eating disorder.

Rock Bottom and the Hospital Journey

Our close friend was dying. The bond between him and our boy was special, vibing over music and beats. My son noticed the deterioration and began asking about death. Shamefully, I tried using this to encourage eating: "You need food to stay healthy." It didn't work and probably added anxiety.

That last visit, my five-year-old grabbed my hand. "Mum, Uncle doesn't look good. That's the last time I'll see him, isn't it? Please don't ever get sick. I don't want you to die." Two days later, our friend passed.

The day of our friend's memorial, my son stopped eating. It was tonsillitis again, but this time it was different. This time, even after the infection cleared, the fear remained.

Twenty-two days of no solid food. Our doctor sent us straight to the children's hospital with instructions: don't leave without answers or a tonsillectomy plan. The hospital stay was intense, specialists puzzled by this articulate five-year-old, surviving on strawberry Up & Go alone. He'd whisper, "Hey, Mum, how about you eat it and tell them I did so we can leave?"

Day five, everything changed. We sat with one of the many specialists our son had seen, and she informed us that the team was unanimous with their diagnosis: ARFID. Avoidant/restrictive food intake disorder. That expulsion of breath was three years of stress, worry, research, and being called crazy, all released at once. Finally, we were seen. Finally, we were heard. Finally, we could really help him.

Lesson Four: Push for proper assessment. Don't accept "picky eater" labels if your gut says otherwise. Document everything: foods dropped, anxiety symptoms, physical responses. Demand referrals to feeding teams. A proper diagnosis isn't just validation; it's the gateway to appropriate support services and understanding from schools.

Finding Creative Solutions in Unexpected Places

We were referred to a child and youth mental health service and fast-tracked due to his age. Weekly family therapy began with a softly spoken, incredibly calm therapist. My son connected immediately, though he warned me: "I'm not listening if she mentions food."

A breakthrough came from an unexpected source – my mother. She created a tent using sheets and a clothes rack, laid placemats on the floor, and served dinner there. No forcing, no pressure, just chatting together in this safe place. He took his first bites in months. My mum had cracked the code: remove traditional meal setting, create novelty and safety. Child's play.

We went wild with mealtime creativity: Cushions on the floor with candlelight. Outdoor picnics. Share plates at the kitchen table. Some worked temporarily; others failed immediately. Every child's key is different.

During a Bali trip (booked on a whim because our dying friend said, "Live your life"), I filled a suitcase with safe foods, including 18 strawberry Up & Gos. He consumed them within three days. Panic set in until I discovered the power of community.

Moments after posting in a Bali family travel group, dozens of parents offered to bring supplies from Australia. Then someone revealed that one supermarket on the island stocked Up & Go. I filled a trolley like a madwoman. But more importantly, I learned I wasn't alone. These parents understood without judgement.

> Lesson Five: Throw conventional wisdom out the window. Meals don't need tables. Food doesn't need plates. If eating under a blanket fort works, do it. If they'll only eat while watching specific shows, let them. If a stuffed animal "tries it first", embrace it. What seems ridiculous to some might be your breakthrough. Seek help. Your tribe exists, and they're waiting to support you.

Seven Truths Every ARFID Parent Must Know

1. You cannot force, bribe, shame, or logic an ARFID child into eating. Anxiety, not defiance, drives behaviour. Release yourself from the burden of "making" them eat.

2. Celebrate microscopic wins: one lick of a new food – progress. Tolerating it on their plate – huge. Adding a safe food deserves a party. You'll lose foods and gain them back repeatedly.

3. Your child thrives despite ARFID. My son remained social, energetic, and creative. His blood work stayed normal. ARFID doesn't define them; it's just one challenge they face.

4. Find your tribe, online or local. Support is life-changing. Seek out other ARFID families. They'll move mountains to help because they've been where you are.

5. Protect their confidence fiercely. Plan school events, family dinners, and birthday parties carefully. True friends won't judge; those who do aren't worth your energy.

6. Supplements and safe foods save lives. During crisis periods, any calorie is a good calorie. Nutrition can be optimised when they're stable.

7. The right therapy is transformative. Some need play therapy, others CBT (cognitive behavioural therapy), others family therapy. The therapist should fit your child, not the other way around.

School Years: Finding Hope in Unexpected Places

Starting school felt impossible. How would he manage six hours without eating? (We had preempted a regression.) What would other kids think? Would the teachers understand? I lay awake creating contingency plans for every scenario. But we chose a school based on its approach to wellness and the well-being of its students.

The first weeks were rough. My son wouldn't eat there, initially surviving only on Up & Go until he got home, then he would eat. We had already educated his teacher and fellow staff members, so they never made a big deal over it.

Then he found his person, a quirky, wonderful boy who didn't judge my son for his liquid-only lunch. They bonded over their love of nature, playgrounds, and collecting random treasures, never food. Their friendship helped pave the way for a more peaceful transition into school. Having each other created a safe place for them to be their authentic selves and gave him his confidence back. We eventually added three safe snacks to his lunchbox alongside the drink. Week by week, less came home. Some weeks, he'd eat everything; others, nothing. The unpredictability continues, but the trajectory is upward.

He joined parkour (who knew he'd find a sport he loved?), where they focus on disciplined training involving movements like running, climbing, and jumping to get from A to B in the most effective way possible. He attends an after-school STEM program that incorporates science, engineering, math, and experiments. Thriving and meeting new friends, all just as quirky as he.

Recently, he announced he was ready for "the robot", a spinning wheel my carpenter husband lovingly built that randomly selects foods to try. We've had it for months, gathering dust while he processed the idea. He's not ready to use it yet, but occasionally spins it and tells me what foods he will "eventually" eat.

With school came questions from curious kids: "Why do you only drink lunch?" "How come you don't eat birthday cake?" He was well-versed and would give simple explanations, which most kids accepted and moved on.

We even managed school excursions with ease, although strategic planning was required: packing safe foods, coordinating with teachers, and preparing him for food-centred activities. Each successful outing built resilience.

Where We Stand Now: In the Light

At six years old, we're not recovered, but we're recovering. He understands food fuels his body for parkour flips and STEM challenges. He's gaining weight appropriately, has colour in his cheeks, energy for days, and most importantly – he's happy.

His safe food list remains small, but it exists: a specific brand of pasta, chicken nuggets and hot chips from one restaurant only, strawberry Up & Go, vanilla ice cream, chicken- or cheese-flavoured crackers or crisps, and plain chocolate frogs. And recently, without even thinking about it, he ate a sausage. Some days, he eats; others, he doesn't. We've learned to surf these waves rather than fight them.

When I look back at the mother who cried nightly over wasted dinners, who googled "can children survive on milk alone", who worried about bones and growth and futures, I want to hug her and whisper, "He'll be okay. Different, but okay."

Practical Strategies That Actually Work

- **Food Presentation Matters:** Some children prefer foods separated, never touching. Our boy was more shape-specific (always squares for sandwiches and crust cut off, never triangles). This increased his acceptance. Familiar packaging and having it visible helped – he needed to see the "safe" brand.
- **Timing is Everything:** Avoid new foods during stressful periods, such as illness, school changes, or family upheaval. Choose calm moments or even proud moments in time.

- **The "Learning Plate":** We introduced a small plate beside his meal for him to look at new foods. No pressure to taste, touch, or smell – just coexist.
- **Safe Food Security:** Always have backup foods available. Running out creates panic that sets progress back weeks. We buy in bulk – yes, it's expensive. His health is worth more.
- **Screen Time Strategy:** We embraced eating while watching shows. Distraction sometimes bypasses anxiety. He's more likely to absent-mindedly munch on snacks while absorbed in Minecraft videos than sitting at a formal table. Judge if you want – it works.
- **Supplement Creativity:** Plain supplements were rejected, but mixed into "special smoothies" with exact ratios of strawberry milk, they became acceptable.

A Letter to You, Fellow Warrior

Those who have 3 a.m. moments googling "ARFID recovery stories", desperately seeking hope, this is for you. You're not crazy. You're not a bad parent because you can't fulfil the basic obligation of feeding your child. You're a warrior fighting an invisible battle that most people can't comprehend.

Your child's future is bright. Celebrations involving food may be difficult, but they'll find their way. They'll develop coping strategies, find understanding friends, possibly expand their foods, and learn to navigate their world.

To every parent who's been told they're "too anxious" and "making it worse", your concern is valid. To everyone hiding their child's eating from judgemental relatives, you're protecting, not enabling. To those whose partners don't understand why you can't "just make them eat", keep educating and advocating.

We've journeyed from complete isolation to a village of support. From doctors who'd never heard of ARFID to a specialised team that truly sees us. From educators who traumatised to those who accommodate beautifully. From my son eating about 15 foods to none to currently about ten.

The path isn't linear; it's spiral. Sometimes you're moving backward to eventually leap forward. Every setback teaches resilience. Every small victory builds confidence. Every day you both survive, your strength reserves grow.

Remember: your child can have ARFID and still have a full, joy-filled life. They can make friends, excel academically, find passions, and contribute meaningfully. ARFID is part of their story, not their entire book.

Our boy will go on to do the greatest things – maybe differently than I once imagined, but great nonetheless. So will yours. This isn't the ending of the story; it's the beginning of understanding, acceptance, and a different kind of hope. Not hope for "normal" but hope for "thriving in their own unique way".

Stay strong, seek support, trust your instincts, and remember, you're not alone in this – we're all out here, fighting similar battles, celebrating tiny victories, and believing in better days ahead.

Watch this space. The best chapters are yet to be written.

We are here to support you.

About Eating Disorders Families Australia

Eating Disorders Families Australia (EDFA) was founded by Australian parents caring for a child with an eating disorder. While our work began with parents, our community has grown to include all those who care for and support someone with an eating disorder, such as partners, siblings, grandparents, extended family members, and friends.

EDFA exists to support, inform, and empower carers through lived-experience connection, trusted information, meaningful EDucation, and strong advocacy. We understand the complexity of caring for someone with an eating disorder and recognise that no two journeys are the same. For this reason, we take a respectful, unbiased approach to treatment models, clinicians, and pathways of care.

As the national voice for eating-disorder carers, our services include peer support through facilitated online groups and a private carer forum, education webinars and information sessions, a prevention and early intervention programs, and access to free counselling support.

Lived experience, hope, and a steadfast belief that recovery is possible are the foundation of everything we do.

An Overview of EDFA Support Programs and Services

Support Program

Carer support groups

Private online carer forum

Support for Siblings

Hospital Liason Officer

EDucation Program

Online information sessions

Clinician subscription service

Nourish, Nurture, Notice prevention program

Strong Enough podcast

Online Counselling Program

Fill The Gap lived-experience counsellors

Young supporters counselling (for those aged 10-18)

Collaborative Care Skills Workshops (CCSW)

List of Resources

Diagnosis to Do List

Step-by-step guide on how to prepare for and then navigate the early days of caring for someone with an eating disorder. https://edfa.org.au/diagnosis-to-do-list/

Sibling Resource Kit

EDFA recognises the challenges facing siblings of those living with an eating disorder and provides support via three toolkits. Available in hard copy or at https://edfa.org.au/siblings-support-2/

Fill The Gap Counselling Program

FREE essential access to tailored, online, one-on-one counselling support for carers and young supporters (aged 10+) of those with eating disorders, at any stage of the eating disorder journey. https://edfa.org.au/fill-the-gap/

Support Program

Join an online support group to connect with other carers of a loved one with an eating disorder Australia-wide. https://edfa.org.au/parents-and-carer-support/eating-disorder-support-groups/

EDucation Program

Twice-monthly Information Sessions for families and carers of individuals with eating disorders, accessible via EDFA membership. https://edfa.org.au/video-resource-library/

EDFA Membership

Become a member and receive a welcome pack, access to EDucation sessions, and much more.
https://edfa.org.au/become-a-member/

Nourish, Nurture, Notice Prevention & Early Identification Program

Australia's first-ever FREE online program focused on the early identification of disordered eating to prevent eating disorders in school-aged children and young people.
https://edfa.org.au/nourish-nurture-notice/

The Strong Enough Podcast

An audio resource where EDFA speaks to research leaders, specialists in education, advocacy, and self-care, as well as individuals with lived experience who share their challenges and successes during the eating disorder recovery journey.
https://edfa.org.au/blog/strong-enough-podcast/

For further information or to enquire about hard copies of any EDFA resources, please email admin@edfa.org.au or phone 1300 195 626.

Visit our website to find out more.

www.ingramcontent.com/pod-product-compliance
Lightning Source LLC
Chambersburg PA
CBHW051806050726
47598CB00006B/2444